DECORATING
COOKIES

60+ DESIGNS FOR HOLIDAYS, CELEBRATIONS & EVERYDAY

Bridget Edwards

LARK CRAFTS
Asheville

Editor
Beth Sweet

Art Director
Kristi Pfeffer

Junior Designer
Meagan Shirlen

Photographer
Steve Mann

Cover Designer
Kristi Pfeffer

An Imprint of Sterling Publishing
387 Park Avenue South
New York, NY 10016

If you have questions or comments about
this book, please visit: larkcrafts.com

Library of Congress Cataloging-in-Publication Data

Edwards, Bridget.
  Decorating cookies : 60+ designs for holidays, celebrations & everyday / Bridget Edwards.
      p. cm.
  Includes index.
  ISBN 978-1-4547-0321-1 (pbk. : alk. paper)
  1. Cookies. 2. Sugar art. 3. Icings, Cake. 4. Food presentation. I. Title.
  TX772.E33 2012
  641.86'54--dc23

                                  2012003890

10 9 8 7 6 5 4 3 2 1

First Edition

Published by Lark Crafts
An Imprint of Sterling Publishing Co., Inc.
387 Park Avenue South, New York, NY 10016

Distributed in Canada by Sterling Publishing,
c/o Canadian Manda Group, 165 Dufferin Street
Toronto, Ontario, Canada M6K 3H6

Distributed in the United Kingdom by GMC Distribution Services,
Castle Place, 166 High Street, Lewes, East Sussex, England BN7 1XU

Distributed in Australia by Capricorn Link (Australia) Pty Ltd.,
P.O. Box 704, Windsor, NSW 2756 Australia

ISBN 13: 978-1-4547-0321-1

For information about custom editions, special sales, and premium and corporate purchases, please contact
Sterling Special Sales Department at 800-805-5489 or specialsales@sterlingpub.com.

Requests for information about desk and examination copies available to college and university professors
must be submitted to academic@larkbooks.com. Our complete policy can be found at www.larkcrafts.com.

CONTENTS

continued on next page

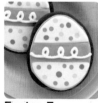

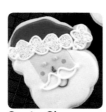

Today's
MENU
_____
• cookies
• cookies
• more cookies

Have you ever gazed into a bakery case at the decorated cookies and thought, "*How* did they *do* that?" I'm here to tell you, it's actually easier than you might think. (It's also highly addictive, so don't say I didn't warn you.) With a few tips, tools, and recipes, you'll be on your way to creating beautiful cookies at home.

Decorated cookies are the perfect sweet treat. First, they are equally appropriate for an elegant wedding reception or a school bake sale. Second, if you make a mistake, you can eat it. Third, you can taste-test a cookie before giving it as a gift (try that with a cake). Fourth, cookies are easily packed, transported, and shipped. And fifth, everyone loves cookies (that's a fact)!

In 1999, I left my job to stay home with my baby boy. I had two goals: to be a good mom and to learn to decorate cookies. Well, I'm not quite sure I've figured out this whole parenting thing, but I have learned a thing or two about cookie decorating. I'm not a pastry chef; I taught myself through lots of trial and error, and I'm so excited to share with you what I've learned.

In this book, you'll find all of the how-to's you need to get creative with cookie decorating. You'll learn about outlining, flooding, and piping with royal icing. We'll use sanding sugar, sprinkles, and luster dust—oh my! Let's not forget the recipes: I've included my very favorite, go-to, never-fail, cut-out cookie recipe, along with a few new cookie flavors you'll want to try.

Also, I'll be introducing you to some of my fabulous cookie-decorator friends, and they're each sharing one of their specialties, from decorating cakes with cookies to reimagining your everyday cookie cutters.

The cookies you'll find inside aren't fancy, complicated, or perfect. Perfection is overrated, don't you think? You'll find a bit of everything here, from a simple one-color "starter" cookie to cookies adorned with luster dust and edible images. (Yes, Virginia, there is a food coloring printer.)

I'll walk you through the techniques and offer helpful hints throughout the Basics section, and in the back of the book, you'll find templates for custom cookie designs and signature embellishments. In between, more than 60 decorated cookie designs are shown in detail to inspire you.

My goal is that you'll learn the techniques to create and decorate cookies that will make your heart go pitter-patter, cookies that you'll want to share with everyone you know, cookies that are delicious and adorable.

The cookie possibilities are endless! Grab your mixer and apron, and let's get baking!

COOKIE DECORATING BASICS

 Equipment and Supplies

To decorate cookies, you'll need a few supplies. Hopefully, you'll find that you have most of them in your kitchen already. Go ahead, stock up and keep them on hand. When the cookie-making mood strikes you, it will save you a dash out to the store for supplies like parchment paper.

Stand Mixer with Paddle Attachment

The dough for decorated cookies is stiff, and beating royal icing (page 28) can take 10 minutes or more. A good stand mixer quickly becomes a cookie maker's best friend. Yes, they are pricier than a hand mixer, but divide that out by the batches of cookies and icing you'll make and it's a great investment. You'll need a paddle attachment for both the cookie dough and the royal icing. Be sure to use an attachment that is sturdy; the one that comes with the mixer is usually best.

Cookie Cutters and Templates

Cookie cutters come in all shapes, sizes, and materials. My favorites range from 3 to 5 inches. A few minis are always fun to have on hand as well. Keep in mind that cookie cutters are multitaskers. Could that candy-corn cutter also be made into a party hat? Could shapes cut with daisy and circle cutters be combined to make a turkey? Yes!

Most of the cookie cutter shapes in this book are commercially available (see Resources on page 159). Some are made from templates I created, which are included on page 156. When you start inventing your own designs and can't find the cookie cutter shape you need, make a template of your own. Simply trace the shape onto something study, such as a piece of cardstock. If you want a permanent, washable template, use a sheet of plastic designed for making quilt templates.

Once your shape is traced and cut, use a small paring knife to cut the dough, using the template as a guide. The shape will be rough around the edges compared to one cut with a cookie cutter. Lightly press the edges with your finger to smooth them.

Icing Tips and Couplers

For cookie decorating, you'll need only three decorating tips to start. They are referred to as "plain tips" and you'll need them in #1, #2, and #3 sizes. The #2 tip is the one I use most often for outlining. For a thicker outline (and for beginners), a #3 tip is perfect. Adding small details or writing with icing? A #1 tip is your best bet.

Having several of each size tip is a good idea. When you have a project that calls for using a tip with four different colors, you won't have to wash that one tip over and over between each color. Using a plastic coupler allows you to switch between tip sizes while keeping the same icing bag (details on page 15).

As you get into the cookie-decorating groove, you may want to pick up a few specialty tips. A handful of projects in the book call for tips other than #1, #2, or #3, such as larger plain tips, star tips, and a basket weave. Be sure to read through the supply list for the projects before starting.

Small tip brushes are available for cleaning. Place the icing tips and couplers in a glass of warm, soapy water. Let them soak for a few minutes, then use the tip brush to clean. Rinse with water until clear. Set them aside to dry or put them on a cookie sheet and place in a 175°F oven for 10 minutes. Let them cool before handling.

Disposable Icing Bags

No more scrubbing bags between icing colors, or exploding sandwich bags! Disposable pastry bags are both convenient and sturdy. Whether you buy a box of 12, 24, or 100, be sure to have these in your cookie-decorating arsenal. Reusable bags are also available, but because they are a challenge to clean, I prefer the disposable option.

Measuring Cups and Spoons

You should have two types of measuring cups for baking: a single measuring cup for liquids, and a set

Ⓐ Cookie cutters in an assortment of shapes, sizes, and materials; Ⓑ Wood (at left) and silicone (at right) rolling pins; Ⓒ A cookie spatula, silicone spatulas, and a sifter; Ⓓ Measuring cups and spoons; Ⓔ A disposable icing bag, plastic couplers, decorating tips in #1, #2, and #3, and a small tip cleaning brush

of individual (often nested) cups for dry measures. Having multiple sets available is always handy. The same goes for measuring spoons—have several sets, so you don't have to stop and wash dishes while baking.

Rolling Pin
Wood or silicone, it doesn't matter. Whichever you like best will work for rolling cookie dough.

Waxed Paper
Used as a rolling surface, waxed paper helps prevent cookie dough from sticking to countertops and makes for easy cleanup.

Parchment Paper
Quite simply, I won't make cookies without it. Parchment paper comes on a roll and can be cut to fit any size cookie sheet. It keeps cookies from sticking and burning, and it doesn't get sticky the way silicone mats can. Parchment can also be reused; it's not necessary to use a fresh sheet with every batch. Find it in the grocery store near the aluminum foil.

Plastic Wrap
Because royal icing dries so quickly, pressing a piece of plastic wrap down onto the icing is a must.

Cookie Sheets
My favorite cookie sheets (also called baking sheets) are the sturdy, light-colored sheets usually labeled as "nonstick." Dark cookie sheets can cause overbrowning, and heavy-duty commercial-grade sheets can lead to cookies that are too soft on the bottom and break easily. The 11 x 17-inch size fits six large cookies with ease. If you have

a side-by-side refrigerator, a smaller sheet is handy for placing cookies in the freezer before baking.

Cooling Racks
Wire cooling racks are essential for cooling cookies. Short on space? Look for racks that are stackable.

Cookie Spatula
Made of very thin metal, a cookie spatula easily slides right underneath cookies to lift them off the cookie sheet without breakage.

Silicone Spatulas
Have a few sizes on hand for stirring icing and scraping cookie dough.

Sifter
For lump-free royal icing, a sifter is a must. To avoid hand cramps, look for one with a turn crank rather than a squeeze trigger.

Assorted Bowls
Royal icing tends to dry out very quickly. Bowls with lids are handy to prevent drying and for storage. Ramekins (small bowls) typically used for food preparation are useful for mixing luster dust or for applying add-ons. Pouring a small amount of sprinkles from a ramekin is easier to manage than pouring directly from the container.

Tall Glasses
For holding piping bags while working, tall glasses do the trick.

Twist Ties
To prevent royal icing from squeezing out the top of a piping bag, or from drying out and getting flaky,

use a twist tie to secure the icing. Place one at the top of the icing and one at the very top of the bag (see page 15).

Squeeze Bottles
Plastic squeeze bottles are perfect for use with flood icing (icing thinned for filling in outlines). The 8- and 16-ounce sizes will work for most any project. Also available are squeeze bottles with removable tips, useful when a more precise application is needed, such as when making small dots or filling a small area. Squeeze bottles can be found in the candy-making section of most craft stores.

Toothpicks
From guiding icing into edges, to popping air bubbles, to scraping off mistakes, toothpicks are my favorite cookie-decorating tool. The round variety has pointy ends, perfect for popping bubbles. Buy the big box.

Dish Towels
These are a must in my kitchen for keeping flood icing from drying and for wiping up messy spills.

It's helpful to make a sketch of your cookie design before starting a new project.

Small Scissors

Designate a small pair of scissors for cookie decorating. Scissors make quick work of trimming edible image sheets.

Small Paintbrushes

Children's bristled paintbrushes are perfect for applying luster dust and prepping cookies for sanding sugar. Make sure they're used only in the kitchen.

Tweezers

One more household item to use exclusively in the kitchen, tweezers are perfect for placing sprinkles, dragées, and nonpareils in exactly the right place.

Bench Scraper

This kitchen tool is usually used to scrape the "bench," or countertop, when working with bread dough. It is the best tool for dividing dough and cutout shapes, such as the circus elephant/pedestal design on page 48.

Paper and Colored Pencils

Before starting a new cookie project, it's helpful to make a sketch of the design. Not only will sketching the cookie design help you visualize the decorating process, but it will also be especially useful in planning icing colors and amounts.

Basket-style Coffee Filter

A coffee filter is invaluable for catching sanding sugar and sprinkles and for funneling excess sprinkles back into their containers.

Paper Towels

Cookie decorating can get messy. You'll need them.

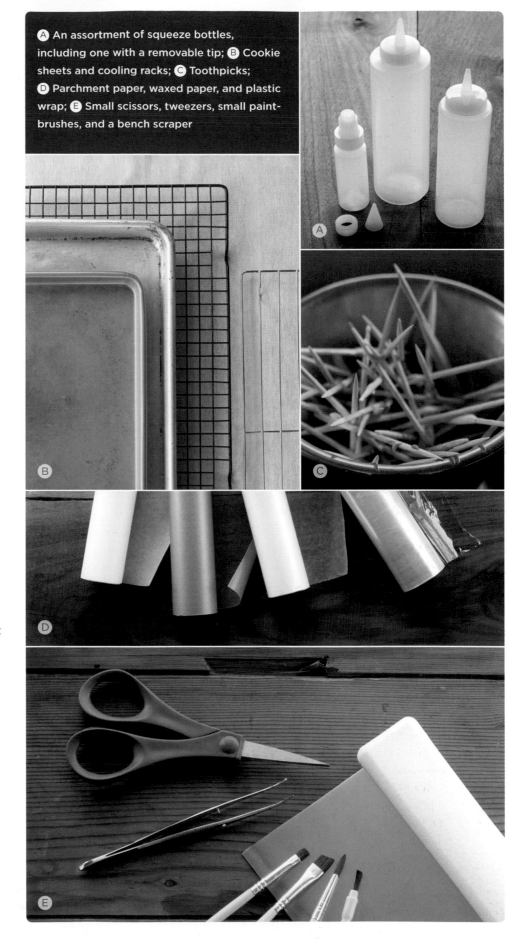

Ⓐ An assortment of squeeze bottles, including one with a removable tip; Ⓑ Cookie sheets and cooling racks; Ⓒ Toothpicks; Ⓓ Parchment paper, waxed paper, and plastic wrap; Ⓔ Small scissors, tweezers, small paintbrushes, and a bench scraper

A Sanding sugar (left) and sparkling sugar (right); B Vanilla bean paste and meringue powder; C An assortment of sprinkles, non-pareils, jimmies, and dragées; D Gel paste food colorings and food-coloring pens; E from left to right: gold luster dust, white disco dust, and red disco dust

Specialty Ingredients

All of the specialty ingredients you'll need can be found at kitchen supply shops, at craft stores, and online. Some, such as meringue powder, are required. Others, such as hot pink disco dust, are optional. This is where the fun begins! Be careful—you may soon end up with an entire shelf in your cabinet devoted to sprinkles, sparkling sugar, and the like. Not that there's anything wrong with that.

Meringue Powder

Royal icing (page 27) can be made with egg whites, powdered egg whites, or meringue powder; I use meringue powder. It's always in my pantry, saving me the worry about using raw eggs or reconstituting powdered egg whites. Although it can be easily found in craft stores and some grocery stores, try buying meringue powder from a bakery or kitchen supply shop for the best taste and results.

Extracts

For royal icing, you'll want to use a clear extract for flavoring. Any dark extracts will tint the icing ever so slightly. Look for extracts labeled as "pure" and, even then, read the label to avoid preservatives, corn syrup, and added sugars.

Vanilla Bean Paste

This is my secret ingredient for fancy-looking cookies. Vanilla bean paste comes in a jar and is a thick liquid filled with flecks of vanilla bean seeds. Use it just as you would vanilla extract. Look for it in your grocery store, at a kitchen supply shop, or online.

Gel Paste Food Colorings

Gel paste food colorings are a must for cookie decorating. They are thick, so they won't change the consistency of your icing, and with just a few drops, they create rich, vivid colors. My favorite food colorings come in squeeze bottles and are easily found online and in bakery and kitchen supply shops.

Food-Coloring Pens

Used to draw and write on royal icing once it's dry, food-coloring pens are wonderful to have on hand. Thinner tips are nice for writing and adding details, while the thicker tips are a good choice for kids to use. You'll find sets in a rainbow of colors, but be sure to have a couple of black pens for common uses, such as drawing eyes (and eyelashes) and personalizing cookies.

Sanding Sugar and Sparkling Sugar

I love adding a little sugar sparkle to my cookies. Despite its name, sparkling sugar is coarser grained and a little less sparkly than sanding sugar.

Sprinkles, Nonpareils, Jimmies, and Dragées

Once you start cookie decorating, you may find yourself collecting cookie add-ons. Not happy with a cookie design? Cover it in sprinkles; everything looks cute with sprinkles!

Luster Dust

When it's brushed on dry, luster dust leaves a sheer metallic sheen. When it's painted on, it gives an opaque metallic shine (details on page 20).

Disco Dust

Also known as fairy dust or pixie dust, disco dust gives an intense sparkle and prismatic effect to cookies. (See the dragonfly cookies on page 42.)

Note: Although metallic add-ons are labeled as nontoxic, the FDA has approved them only for decorative use. Do I eat them? Yes. Do I consume the entire jar in one sitting? No. Use your best judgment and do what feels comfortable to you.

Disco dust adds intense sparkle to decorated cookies.

Techniques

Once you have the supplies, go ahead and bake a batch of cookies and mix up some royal icing (see page 28). Now you're ready to start decorating! Every trick that you need to know to make beautifully decorated cookies is right here. Really! Refer back to this section as you're working. You'll find cookie examples of each one of these techniques throughout the book.

Setting Up Your Work Surface

Once the cookies are baked and completely cooled, transfer them back to cookie sheets for decorating. I love using cookie sheets because they make the cookies easily portable and manageable. Place the cookies along the edges of the sheets, leaving the middle empty, so you're not reaching over one row of cookies to decorate another.

Tinting Royal Icing

Coloring icing is easy! Just add gel paste colors to your icing and stir. Colors will become deeper when they sit for a while, especially dark colors; so, when tinting icing a color such as red, black, or brown, bring the icing almost to the color you want and stop. As it dries, the icing will darken to the perfect shade. Oversaturation can lead to bleeding colors.

When mixing different shades of the same color, such as the two grays for the robot cookies on page 54, start adding color for the lightest shade by dipping a toothpick into the food coloring and then into the icing (use a fresh toothpick for each dip). Gel paste colors are highly concentrated, so sometimes just a bit does the trick. For the darker shade, divide the icing and add more coloring. Specific amounts will depend on how much icing you have to tint.

Color Planning

Before making a new cookie design, I always sketch out the design and color it in with colored pencils. Then, I make a note of which colors I'll need and whether I need them for outlining, flooding, or both. This helps me plan how much I'll need of each color.

The same goes for following one of the projects in the book. Read it through before you start, look at the cookies, and eyeball which colors you'll need more of. The instructions will say to "divide and tint," but I don't list specific amounts for each color. Sometimes you only need a little bit of one color, such as black icing for the eyes. This is a creative process, and you're the artist! Do what works for you.

The colors listed in the project instructions are based on the gel paste brand I use, but they are also descriptive enough to steer you in the right direction. (Any brand you choose is fine.) For instance, I use four shades of pink in this book, and I call them deep pink, soft pink, electric pink, and rose pink. Just go by the photographs and use your best creative judgment. You might want to use completely different colors than the ones I used.

Before making the icing, set out different-size bowls and place a strip of paper next to each one to remind you which color goes into it. A little extra planning will really help, and it will keep you from ending up with a big bowl of purple when what you really needed was white. For the most part, you can use the colors straight out of the bottle, but occasionally I will suggest that you mix two different colors together. (If you're having trouble with your icing, see Troubleshooting on page 29.)

> **TIP** *Red and black icings are notorious for being difficult to color. Either they require vast amounts of coloring (to get past pink and gray) or they leave a not-so-pleasant aftertaste. Here is where you'll want to use a high-quality gel paste coloring. Depending on how much icing you're coloring, just a few squeezes will do. Look for red and black coloring marked as "super" at a bakery supply shop, rather than the craft store. If there is no bakery supply shop in your town, try ordering online.*

Using a Coupler and Tips

To use a coupler and tips with a pastry bag:

1 Insert the tube part of the coupler into the bag as far as it will go. Cut the bag just beneath where the coupler ends Ⓐ.

Note: The instructions on the box will tell you to cut it up near the threads. I've had too many bags leak this way. Cut farther down to prevent this.

2 Place the tip you'd like to use on the end of the tube (on top of the bag). Attach the ring part of the coupler to secure Ⓑ.

3 To easily change tips while decorating, unscrew the coupler ring, switch the tips, and then reattach the ring.

Filling a Piping Bag

Once your coupler and tip are in place, you're ready to fill your piping bag with icing.

1 Open the top of the bag and fold it to the outside by several inches to make a cuff. Hold the piping bag with one hand under the cuff.

2 With the other hand, use a silicone spatula to scoop royal icing out of the bowl Ⓒ. Fill the bag half to two-thirds full at the most.

3 Fold the cuff back up, twist, and secure with a twist tie at the top of the icing and at the top of the bag Ⓓ.

> **FYI** *Why Do I Need a White Tint for Icing?* **It sounds crazy, because fresh royal icing looks perfectly white, but do use a white food coloring. Plain, untinted white icing has a tendency to dry into a dull off-white. As a matter of fact, use more white tint than you think you need to ensure a white-white cookie.**

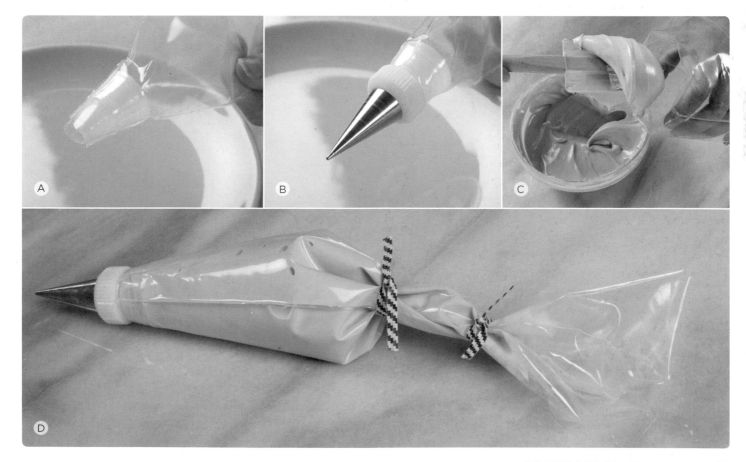

Basic Piping for Outlining

For basic outlining and piping, hold your piping bag in your dominant hand at the top of the icing. Hold the bag at an angle above the cookie Ⓐ, squeeze the bag from the top, and use your other hand to guide the bag along. Make sure the tip is above the cookie, not touching it Ⓑ.

If you're like I was, your hand may be a bit shaky when you first start learning. As with everything, you'll feel more confident with practice. Before starting on a cookie, practice a bit on a plate or a sheet of waxed paper.

Thinning Royal Icing for Flooding

This is probably the trickiest part of cookie decorating and the part that scares most people. The goal is to thin the icing to the consistency of a thick syrup. Don't be scared! If I can figure it out, so can you!

1 Start with a bowl of tinted royal icing and a small cup of room-temperature water. Add the water to the icing a bit at a time. Depending on how much icing you have to thin, you may want to start with a tablespoon or a teaspoon. I normally start with a teaspoon or two of water Ⓒ.

2 Stir with a silicone spatula after each addition of water. Using a mixer will add too many air bubbles, so be sure to stir by hand Ⓓ. Keep adding water, decreasing the increments as you get closer to the right consistency. At that point, even a few drops of water will make a difference.

3 Bring the spatula up and drop a "ribbon" of icing back into the bowl and start counting Ⓔ. You're looking for it to disappear in a count of "one-thousand-one, one-thousand-two." If the ribbon takes longer to disappear, keep adding water. If it disappears too quickly, stir in some sifted powdered sugar.

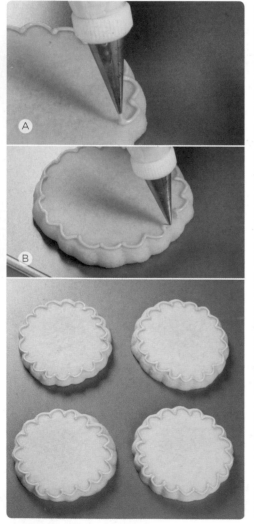

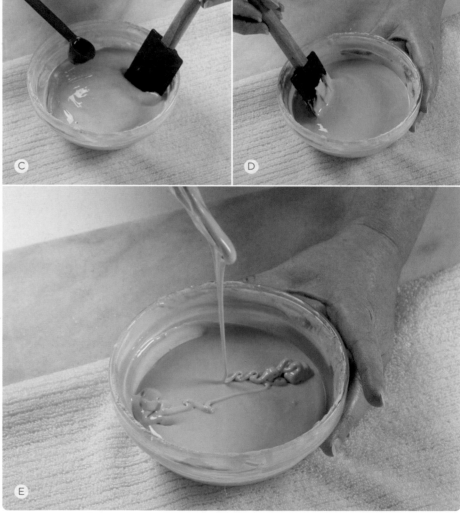

4 Once the icing has reached the desired consistency, cover it with a damp dish towel and let it sit for several minutes. This will allow large air bubbles to rise to the top. Stir gently with a silicone spatula, transfer to a squeeze bottle, and you're ready to go.

Note: Adding water to royal icing for thinning will not change the color.

Flooding

Flooding cookies is just a fancy term for filling in an outline with thinned icing. Fill a squeeze bottle with thinned icing Ⓕ and simply squeeze onto the outlined cookie. Go around the edges, and then go back and forth or up and down to fill in the targeted area Ⓖ. Don't worry about covering the cookie perfectly; the icing will spread into empty spaces.

I typically flood three cookies at a time. Working a few cookies at a time gives the icing a minute or so to spread on its own. Once the cookies are flooded, go back with a toothpick and guide the icing into empty places and edges Ⓗ. The cookie should not be visible through the icing. If it looks too thin, just add some more. Use the point of a toothpick to pop any air bubbles.

Detail Piping

Straight Lines. Hold the piping bag at an angle in your dominant hand and guide with your other hand, keeping the tip above the cookie Ⓘ. Start at one end and look toward the end point, pulling the icing along Ⓙ. Avoid dragging it across the cookie or touching the cookie with the icing tip.

Centering Names. When personalizing a cookie, I always start with the center letter. First, write the name on a piece of paper just to be sure you have it correct. Find the center letter, or two center letters, and pipe those first in the middle of the cookie, working out to the ends. This method works for printed letters, not cursive.

Getting Dotty (Making Flat Dots)

Ah, one of the mysteries of cookie decorating: how to get those flat dots in the icing? It's so easy.

1 Outline the cookie, then thin two (or more) colors of icing for flooding. Be sure to thin them to the same consistency. Transfer the icing to squeeze bottles.

2 Working on six to eight cookies at a time, flood the cookie with the base color. Guide the icing to the edges with a toothpick and pop any air bubbles.

3 Go back to the first cookie that was filled; this gives the base coat time to set a bit. Drop dots straight onto the wet icing with the second color Ⓐ.

Note: This also works for flat stripes.

Marbling

A marbling effect is achieved much the same way as making flat dots.

1 Outline the cookie and then thin two (or more) colors of icing for flooding. Be sure to thin the icings to the same consistency. Transfer the icing to squeeze bottles.

2 Working on six to eight cookies at a time, flood the cookie with the base color. Guide the icing to the edges with a toothpick and pop any air bubbles.

3 Go back to the first cookie that was filled and squeeze lines onto the wet icing Ⓑ.

4 Drag a toothpick through the lines to create swirls or zigzags Ⓒ and Ⓓ.

Embellishing

Embellishing is the term I use for all icing work done ahead of time and then placed on a cookie, such as a monogram, a logo, or a symbol. Make the embellishments at least a day before making the cookies.

1 Locate or resize an image to fit inside the dimensions of the cookie cutter. It's helpful to copy and paste the image several times onto a sheet of paper for tracing.

2 Flip a cookie sheet upside down. Place the printed sheet on the cookie sheet and cover it with a sheet of waxed paper. Tape the waxed paper on two opposite ends to hold it in place Ⓔ.

3 Using royal icing of piping consistency, trace the images onto the waxed paper Ⓕ. For letters and monogramming, a #2 or a #3 tip works best. Images traced with a #1 tip tend to be too fragile. When tracing a logo that needs to be flooded, outline it first, then flood, just like on a cookie.

4 Let the images dry overnight, uncovered, on a counter or tabletop where they won't be disturbed. The next day, gently remove the images, either by folding back the waxed paper or by using a thin metal cookie spatula to slide underneath Ⓖ. If not using the embellishments the same day, store in an airtight container at room temperature.

Note: Make many more embellishments than you will need. Letters, especially ones with lots of flourishes, tend to break when removed from the waxed paper.

There are two ways to apply embellishments. For larger images, simply pipe dots of royal icing onto the back of the image and adhere it to a dry cookie. For smaller embellishments, such as monograms, flood the cookies as usual and let them sit for 30 minutes. Then, very gently, place the monogram onto the cookie Ⓗ. The icing will still be wet enough to hold the image, but it will have set enough to avoid creating an air bubble.

Note: Candy melts (easy-to-melt wafers designed for candymaking and dipping) can also be used for embellishing and are less susceptible to breakage. Keep in mind that the candy melts cannot be colored to exactly match your icing colors.

Using Food-Coloring Pens
Food-coloring pens are one of the easiest ways to decorate cookies. Outline and flood cookies and let

them dry overnight. Once the cookies are dry, decorate with food-coloring pens, using them just like markers. Use a light touch, because the pens can break through the surface of the icing. I use them mostly for making black dot "eyes" and eyelashes on cookies; it's one less icing color to make.

Using Add-ons
I have suspected this for years and now I have proof. I'm a control freak. When applying cookie add-ons, such as sprinkles, jimmies, sanding sugar, and sparkling sugar, I want control. I want to know exactly where they will stick and I don't want icing running all over the place. I also don't like the dents that some sprinkles can leave in wet icing. So, I apply add-ons to dry cookies.

1 Let your cookies dry, uncovered, overnight.

2 Set up an "add-on station." You'll need a paper towel, a basket-style coffee filter, a small paintbrush, and two small ramekins.

3 In one of the ramekins, mix together equal parts meringue powder and water. Start with $1/2$ teaspoon of each, unless you are decorating more than three dozen cookies; in that case, start with 1 teaspoon of each. Fill the other ramekin with the add-ons.

4 Line your work surface with a paper towel. Use the paintbrush to apply the meringue powder mixture onto the targeted cookie area. Hold the cookie over the coffee filter and shake on the sanding sugar, sprinkles, or jimmies. Let the excess fall into the coffee filter. Use the filter as a funnel to pour the add-ons back into the container.

5 The cookies will be set and ready for packaging in 30 minutes or so.

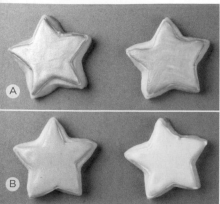

Adding Shine (Luster Dust)

Luster dust can be applied either wet or dry, depending on whether you'd like an opaque or a sheer look.

FOR AN OPAQUE, METALLIC FINISH (A)

1 Mix some luster dust with vodka in a small container. A little luster goes a long way and it doesn't take much vodka to make it liquid. Start with ¼ teaspoon of luster dust and several drops of vodka.

Note: Vodka works best, but if you don't have any on hand, you can use a clear extract, such as lemon. That will, of course, change the flavor of the icing.

2 With a small paintbrush, add luster to the desired area of a dry cookie. The alcohol will evaporate, leaving just the metallic shine. Because the evaporation happens quickly, you'll need to add vodka to your mixture periodically while you work.

Note: The vodka/luster dust mixture can be left to dry once your decorating is finished. All of the alcohol will evaporate and the luster dust can be reused.

FOR A SHEER LOOK (B)

The dry application of luster dust leaves a subtle sheen on finished cookies. Dip a small paintbrush into the container of luster dust and simply brush on dried cookies.

Using Disco Dust

Disco dust makes cookies sparkle like nothing else, but I'll warn you: your cookies won't be the only thing wearing it. You'll find sparkles on your table, on your floor, in your hair, and even on your neighbor's dog (it travels).

I apply disco dust in the same way as other add-ons, but this isn't as precise as adding sanding sugar (C). Because the disco dust particles are so small, stray sparkles tend to stick in places that you didn't intend them to.

Edible Images

Edible images are printed in food coloring "ink" onto thin frosting sheets. Whether you invest in an icing printer of your own or format and take your images to be printed at a bakery supply shop or grocery store bakery, edible-image cookies are really fun for photographs and logos. (Who wouldn't want his or her kindergarten picture printed on a cookie?)

1 Format the image to fit your cookie by cropping and viewing on your computer at 100 percent. Make the image just a bit smaller than the cookie cutter. Copy and paste the image into a document, fitting as many on one page as possible (D). (Most frosting sheets have a printable area of 7½ x 10 inches.) Once printed, edible images should be stored in a large zip-top bag at room temperature.

2 When ready to use, cut the images apart, leaving the backing sheet in place. Outline and flood the cookies, then peel the backing off the image. Gently place the image on the wet icing.

3 Allow the cookies to dry, uncovered, for at least 24 hours. The images can trap the moisture of the wet icing and make the drying process longer.

4 Add a piped star border or a border of sanding sugar or sprinkles (examples on pages 60 and 116) to make the cookies even more special.

Helpful Hints

Practicing

If you're new to decorating cookies, give yourself some time to get comfortable with the process. Practice piping on a plate, experiment with different designs, and don't expect perfection. What you see as mistakes, others will see as cute cookies—I promise. (The projects on pages 30 and 31 are a great place for newbies to start.)

Time

Allow yourself more time than you think you need for decorating; it's no fun if you have to rush. How much time you need will, of course, depends on how many cookies you're making and how complicated the design is. Generally, allow 4 to 5 hours to bake and decorate two dozen cookies with a simple design. (This does not include drying time.) I like to make cookies on one day and decorate them the next to break up the process a bit.

Decorating with Kids

Have everything ready before calling the kids into the kitchen. That means having the cookies on trays, the icings in bags and bottles, and the sprinkles in bowls (lots and lots of sprinkles).

Elevate Your Work Space

My husband looked at me as I was decorating cookies one day and said, "Why don't you raise up your cookie tray?" Brilliant! Use a stool or a stack of cookbooks and get that cookie-decorating tray to a height that is comfortable for you. It makes all the difference in the world!

Starting Over

Sometimes it happens: the cookie doesn't look like you wanted, the outline looks shaky, or you just want to start over. Here's where your friend the toothpick comes in handy. Scrape off the icing and start again!

Cover It Up

You've finished decorating and just aren't happy with the way things turned out. Never fear—it's sanding sugar and sprinkles to the rescue! Repeat after me, "Everything looks cute when covered in sprinkles!" (Instructions for applying add-ons are on page 19.)

Making Extra

If I need 24 cookies, I always make at least 28. If I'm making 24 cookies, I make icing to cover 36. Making extra allows for mistakes, for playing with designs, and for taste-testing. I always like to have a little extra plain icing set aside in case I have misjudged how much I need of a certain color. It beats mixing up a new batch of icing.

Most important, have fun! Yes, you might run into a few snags along the cookie-decorating road, but remember, you are the only one who notices the mistakes. I promise that your friends, your neighbors, and your family will just see your adorable cookies.

COOKIES AND ROYAL ICING

The recipes in this section are not only delicious, but the cookies also hold up well to decorating, packaging, stacking, and shipping. You'll find all of these to be nice, thick, substantial cookies. If you like your cookies more on the crisp side, feel free to roll them out a bit thinner.

Vanilla-Almond Sugar Cookies

Makes 12 to 18 cookies, depending on cookie size

This is my go-to sugar cookie recipe. I could make them in my sleep (and probably have). The real beauty of this recipe is that it doesn't require chilling before rolling. If you want to change it up a bit, I've included some easy variations.

YOU WILL NEED

- 3 cups unbleached, all-purpose flour
- 2 teaspoons baking powder
- 1 cup (2 sticks) salted butter, cold and cut into chunks
- 1 cup sugar
- 1 egg
- 3/4 teaspoon pure vanilla extract
- 1/2 teaspoon pure almond extract

● Position a rack in the center of the oven and preheat the oven to 350°F.

● Line three cookie sheets with parchment paper.

Note: Typically, I bake only six cookies per sheet, spaced approximately 2 inches apart.

● In a medium bowl, whisk together the flour and baking powder. Set this mixture aside.

● In the large bowl of a stand mixer fitted with a paddle attachment, cream together the butter and sugar until combined and fluffy. Beat in the egg and extracts, mixing until combined.

● Add the flour mixture 1 cup at a time, mixing on low speed until just combined. Scrape down the sides and bottom of the bowl as needed. After the last addition, the mixture will look very thick and crumbly.

● Prepare a rolling surface and roll out a portion of the dough (see Rolling and Cutting Cookie Dough at right). Cut as many shapes from the dough as possible and place them onto a prepared cookie sheet.

● Place the cookie sheet in the freezer for 5 to 10 minutes. Freezing the cookies helps them keep their shape while baking. Meanwhile, knead the scraps and remaining dough together and continue the rolling, cutting, and freezing process on a second prepared cookie sheet.

● After freezing, immediately bake the cookies on the center rack of your oven for 9 to 12 minutes, or until they appear done in the center. The cookies will not change much in color and the edges will not brown.

Remove the cookies from the oven and let them cool for 2 minutes on the cookie sheet. With a thin cookie spatula, transfer the cookies to a wire rack to cool completely.

● Rotate the cookie sheets from the freezer to the oven to the cooling rack until all of the cookies are baked.

Variations

Va-Va-Vanilla: Replace the extracts with 2 teaspoons vanilla bean paste.

Vanilla Bean–Almond: Replace the vanilla extract with 1 teaspoon vanilla bean paste.

Lemon: Reduce the vanilla extract to ½ teaspoon. Add ½ teaspoon fresh lemon juice and ¾ teaspoon grated lemon zest.

Plain Jane: Omit both extracts for a cookie that is all buttery-sugary goodness.

Rolling and Cutting Cookie Dough

Do not fear the flour! Flouring your rolling surface, rolling pin, and cookie cutters will make your cookie-decorating life so much easier. Here is my standard procedure.

1 Line your rolling surface with waxed paper. This will help prevent sticking and make for easier cleanup.

2 Dust the surface with flour. Coat your rolling pin in flour Ⓐ.

3 If the dough is sticky or crumbly, roll it on the flour-coated surface and knead it together until smooth. Roll to the desired thickness; I prefer about ¼ inch thick Ⓑ.

4 Dip the cookie cutter in flour and press straight down Ⓒ. Get as many shapes out of one rolled piece of dough as possible Ⓓ.

5 Gather the scraps, and then lift the cut shapes onto a parchment-lined cookie sheet. You can just pick them up with your hand; it's a sturdy dough Ⓔ.

6 Recoat the waxed paper with flour if needed, knead the scraps and remaining dough together, and roll again. Don't worry about overworking the dough.

Note: Some say that powdered sugar is a good substitute for rolling. I find it makes my cookie dough sticky and the tops are not as smooth.

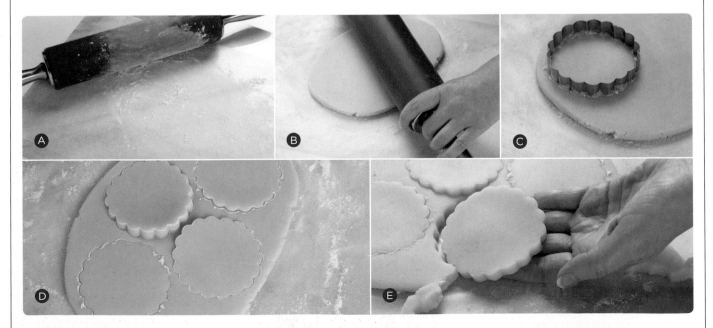

Chocolate-Hazelnut Cookies

Makes 12 to 18 cookies, depending on cookie size

My husband declared these cookies "as close to a brownie as a cookie will ever get." They are decadent. For me, this recipe is a good excuse to always have Nutella in the house! Decorating cookies in pink or yellow? This dark cookie base really makes the colors pop.

YOU WILL NEED

2½ cups unbleached, all-purpose flour

½ cup Dutch-processed cocoa powder

⅛ teaspoon coarse salt

2 teaspoons baking powder

1 cup (2 sticks) salted butter, cold and cut into chunks

1 cup sugar

½ cup Nutella (chocolate-hazelnut spread)

1 egg

1 teaspoon pure vanilla extract

● Position a rack in the center of the oven and preheat the oven to 350°F.

● Line three cookie sheets with parchment paper.

● In a medium bowl, whisk together the flour, cocoa, salt, and baking powder. Set this mixture aside.

● In the large bowl of a stand mixer fitted with a paddle attachment, cream together the butter and sugar until combined and fluffy. Add the Nutella and mix well. Beat in the egg and the vanilla until combined.

● Add the flour mixture in three parts, mixing on low speed, until just combined. Scrape down the sides and bottom of the bowl as needed.

● Divide the dough in half and form into disks. Wrap each disk in plastic wrap, and refrigerate for at least 30 minutes.

● Line the rolling surface with waxed paper (see Rolling and Cutting Cookie Dough on page 23). Mix a bit of flour with cocoa on a plate for rolling and dipping the cookie cutters. Dust the rolling surface and rolling pin with the flour and cocoa mixture.

● Roll out one of the disks and cut as many shapes from the dough as possible. Place the shapes onto a prepared cookie sheet, approximately 2 inches apart.

● Place the cookie sheet in the freezer for 5 to 10 minutes. Freezing the cookies helps them keep their shape while baking. Meanwhile, knead the scraps and remaining dough together and continue the rolling, cutting, and freezing process on a second prepared cookie sheet.

● After freezing, immediately bake the cookies on the center rack for 9 to 12 minutes, or until they appear done in the center.

● Remove the cookies from the oven and let them cool for 2 minutes on the cookie sheet. With a thin cookie spatula, transfer the cookies to a wire rack to cool completely.

● Rotate the cookie sheets from the freezer to the oven to the cooling rack until all of the cookies are baked.

Key Lime Pie Cookies

Makes 12 to 18 cookies, depending on cookie size

Key Lime Pie Cookies are a little unexpected, but the tanginess of the lime is such a hit at a summer picnic—or maybe for Pi Day on March 14th.

YOU WILL NEED

2 3/4 cups unbleached, all-purpose flour

1/3 cup graham cracker crumbs

2 teaspoons baking powder

1 cup (2 sticks) salted butter, cold and cut into chunks

1 cup sugar

1 egg

1 1/2 teaspoons Key lime extract

■ Position a rack in the center of the oven and preheat the oven to 350°F.

■ Line three cookie sheets with parchment paper.

■ In a medium bowl, whisk together the flour, graham cracker crumbs, and baking powder. Set this mixture aside.

■ In the large bowl of a stand mixer fitted with a paddle attachment, cream together the butter and sugar until combined and fluffy. Beat in the egg and Key lime extract, mixing until combined.

■ Add the flour mixture in three parts, mixing on low speed. Scrape down the sides and bottom of the bowl as needed. After the last addition, the mixture will look very thick and crumbly.

■ Prepare a rolling surface and roll out a portion of the dough (see Rolling and Cutting Cookie Dough on page 23). Cut as many shapes from the dough as possible and place them onto a prepared cookie sheet, approximately 2 inches apart.

■ Place the cookie sheet in the freezer for 5 to 10 minutes. Freezing the cookies helps them keep their shape while baking. Meanwhile, knead the scraps and remaining dough together and continue the rolling, cutting, and freezing process on a second prepared cookie sheet.

■ After freezing, immediately bake the cookies on the center rack of your oven for 9 to 12 minutes, or until the cookies appear done in the center. They will not change much in color and the edges will not brown.

■ Remove the cookies from the oven and let them cool for 2 minutes on the cookie sheet. With a thin cookie spatula, transfer the cookies to a wire rack to cool completely.

■ Rotate the cookie sheets from the freezer to the oven to the cooling rack until all of the cookies are baked.

Gingerbread Cookies

Makes 18 to 30 cookies, depending on cookie size

I find myself wanting to make gingerbread all year long—not just in winter! For a warm-weather treat, try sandwiching a mixture of lemon curd and marshmallow cream between two gingerbread cookies. You'll never wait until December again! As far as gingerbread cookies go, I like them thick and chewy. If you like yours a bit crispier, just roll them thinner.

YOU WILL NEED

5½   cups unbleached, all-purpose flour

1½   teaspoons baking soda

½   teaspoon coarse salt

1½   tablespoons ground ginger

2   teaspoons cinnamon

½   teaspoon allspice

¼   teaspoon ground cloves

1   cup (2 sticks) salted butter, cold and cut into chunks

½   cup sugar

½   cup packed light brown sugar

1   cup molasses

1   egg

◼ Position a rack in the center of the oven and preheat the oven to 350°F.

◼ Line three cookie sheets with parchment paper.

◼ In a medium bowl, whisk together the flour, baking soda, salt, ginger, cinnamon, allspice, and cloves. Set this mixture aside.

◼ In the large bowl of a stand mixer fitted with a paddle attachment, cream together the butter and both sugars until light and fluffy. Beat in the molasses and egg. Mix until well combined.

◼ Add the flour mixture in three parts, mixing on low speed until just combined. Scrape down the sides and bottom of the bowl as needed.

◼ Divide the dough in half and form into disks. Wrap each disk in plastic wrap, and refrigerate for at least 30 minutes.

◼ Prepare a rolling surface and roll out one of the disks (see Rolling and Cutting Cookie Dough on page 23). Cut as many shapes from the dough as possible and place them onto a prepared cookie sheet, approximately 2 inches apart.

◼ Place the cookie sheet in the freezer for 5 to 10 minutes. Freezing the cookies helps them keep their shape while baking. Meanwhile, knead the scraps and remaining dough together and continue the rolling, cutting, and freezing process on a second prepared cookie sheet.

◼ After freezing, immediately bake the cookies on the center rack of your oven for 9 to 12 minutes, or until the cookies appear done in the center.

◼ Remove the cookies from the oven and let them cool for 2 minutes on the cookie sheet. With a thin cookie spatula, transfer the cookies to a wire rack to cool completely.

◼ Rotate the cookie sheets from the freezer to the oven to the cooling rack until all of the cookies are baked.

Royal Icing

According to *A Gourmet's Guide: Food and Drink from A to Z*, by John Ayto, the first printed recipe for "icing" appeared in 1769. A version of royal icing was called "Sugar Icing for a Bride Cake" and instructed the baker to beat egg whites and sugar with a knife against a pewter dish for a total of an hour. Now that is dedication!

Royal icing dries hard and opaque, which makes it perfect for decorating, stacking, and packaging. When it comes to icing, my philosophy is, "More is more." Nothing will zap your cookie-decorating mojo like having to stop in the middle of decorating because you've run out of icing.

This recipe will produce enough piping-consistency icing to cover several dozen cookies, depending on the amount of decorative details and colors you create. If you're only decorating one or two dozen cookies in just a couple of colors, feel free to halve this recipe. For flooding, the icing will need to be thinned (see the directions on page 16). If you run into problems with icing that is too thick, too thin, or too flaky, see Troubleshooting on page 29. For color tinting, see page 14.

Cookie Storage

Once baked and cooled, cookies can be kept in an airtight container for a day or two before decorating. Iced cookies are best enjoyed within a week of decorating. Store cookies in individual treat bags for maximum freshness, or place them in an airtight container.

Freezing Cookies

Cookie dough may be frozen for 3 to 6 months. Simply wrap the dough in plastic wrap, seal it in a resealable freezer bag, and freeze. Thaw the dough at room temperature.

Baked cookies may also be frozen. Stack them between layers of waxed paper and place in a resealable freezer bag or plastic container (or both). Even iced cookies can be frozen! I like to individually bag cookies, and then place them in freezer bags. Placing these inside plastic containers ensures that the cookies won't get crushed in the freezer. Thaw the iced cookies at room temperature for several hours in their packaging.

Frozen cookies are best eaten within 6 months, although, just for fun, I once kept some in my freezer for a year and they still tasted great.

Packaging

Individual treat bags are the best bet for cookie packaging. An individually bagged cookie, tied with a ribbon, is a present in itself; the bag keeps the cookie fresh and protects the icing from chipping.

When individually packaging cookies is not an option, layer the cookies between sheets of waxed paper in an airtight container. Remember, never store cookies in the refrigerator. Condensation can ruin the icing.

Shipping

Sending a box of cookies in the mail is one of my favorite things to do. It's also nerve-racking, and quite possibly, hive-inducing. To ship cookies with the least amount of breakage follow these tips.

• Individually bag each cookie and tie the bags with ribbon.

• Layer the cookies in a sturdy, document-style box. Plan on two layers of cookies per box.

• Line each box with a sheet of foam or small bubble wrap. Place a sheet of foam between the cookie layers. Place a sheet of foam on top.

• Close the box and seal with packing tape.

• Place the document boxes inside a larger shipping box. Cushion with packing peanuts.

• Cross your fingers and ship the cookies.

 TIP *Cookies without appendages ship best. Think circles and squares.*

YOU WILL NEED

½ cup meringue powder

1 scant cup water (meaning not quite full)

2 pounds (32 ounces) powdered sugar

2 teaspoons light corn syrup

▮ In the large bowl of a stand mixer fitted with a paddle attachment, mix together the meringue powder and water until foamy and combined.

▮ Sift in the powdered sugar Ⓐ, add the corn syrup Ⓑ, and mix on low speed until the powdered sugar is incorporated. Scrape down the sides and bottom of the bowl with a silicone spatula. Increase the speed to medium-low and beat for 5 minutes Ⓒ.

▮ Increase the mixer's speed to medium-high and continue beating, just until the icing is glossy and stiff peaks form. To check for stiff peaks, take the beater off the mixer and hold it so that the icing is pointing up in the air. If the peak is floppy, keep beating Ⓓ. If the icing holds a point and keeps that point when jiggled, you have a stiff peak Ⓔ.

Note: Be careful not to overbeat the icing, or it might become flaky when applied to the cookie. Keep a close eye on the glossy sheen; overbeating will cause it to go dull.

Flavoring

Plain royal icing deliciously accompanies any cookie, but it can be flavored as well. Choose a flavoring that complements your cookie's taste, and remember to use a clear extract. Dark extracts will tint the icing ever so slightly. Add the following flavors along with the powdered sugar and corn syrup.

Almond: add ½ teaspoon pure almond extract

Lemon: add 2 teaspoons fresh lemon juice

Key Lime: add ½ teaspoon Key lime extract

Icing Storage

Royal icing can be made ahead of time and refrigerated for several days, though it is best to use it the same day you make it. To store icing, be sure to press a piece of plastic wrap down onto its surface, because any exposed icing will dry and crack. You can store leftover icing in the piping bags, as well. The tips may clog, but you can just swap them out or clear them with a toothpick. Leftover piping-consistency icing can be saved and used within a few days, but icing thinned for flooding must be used within a few hours or it will separate.

Stored icing will lose some of its stiffness, so keep that in mind if you're working on very fine details. To thicken stored icing, place it in your mixer, gradually add sifted powdered sugar, and beat the icing with the paddle attachment until stiff peaks form.

Troubleshooting

Sometimes, you might run into a bit of trouble while cookie decorating. How do I know? Each and every one of the issues mentioned here has happened to me. Remember, it's just a cookie. If you make a mistake, cover it in sprinkles or eat it! No one will be the wiser.

Cookie Issues

The cookies are spreading during baking and losing their shape.

To stop the spread, be sure to freeze cookies for 5 to 10 minutes before baking. Place cookies directly into the oven from the freezer without thawing.

The cookies are getting bumpy on top when baked.

First, make sure the cookie dough is fully kneaded together before rolling. Second, about 2 minutes before the baking time is complete, check the cookies for bumps. Lightly press any bumps down with your finger.

The cookie dough is crumbly and falling apart.

Be sure to knead the dough together to make it cohesive and uniform in texture.

The bottoms of the cookies burned before the tops were done.

Check the following: that your oven rack is in the middle position, that the cookie sheet is lined with parchment, and that the cookie sheet itself is a sturdy, light-colored sheet. Also, double-check your oven temperature with an oven thermometer. Oven temperatures can vary widely, even when set correctly.

Icing Issues

The royal icing won't dry, even after 24 hours.

Most likely, the flood icing was thinned a bit too much. (See page 16 for instructions on how to thin icing.)

The royal icing is pitted and sticky after drying overnight.

Oh, this might be the most heartbreaking cookie issue of them all! Your cookies looked perfect when you went to bed, but in the morning, they are pitted and sticky. Again, the flood icing was probably thinned a bit too much. If you have time, scrape the pitted icing out of the outline (use a small spoon), make a new batch of icing, and try again.

The icing dried with dark spots.

This is most common with darker colors and is caused by humidity. In some cases, the dark splotches will spread to cover the entire cookie. While the icing is drying, run the air conditioning or a fan and, by all means, do not open a window on a humid day while the cookies are drying. (My husband learned this the hard way.)

My hands ache after piping cookies.

Fill a piping bag no more than two-thirds full. Also, check the consistency of the icing. If the icing is too stiff, you're pushing harder than you need to when piping. Squeeze the icing back into a bowl, add just a few drops of water to loosen up the icing, and try again.

My hands shake when I'm piping.

Practice, practice, practice—whether it's on a paper towel, a plate, or a cookie sheet.

The royal icing is breaking and popping while I am outlining cookies.

If royal icing is too stiff, it can break during piping. Either go back over the skipped area in the outline, or put all of the icing back into a bowl, add a few drops of water, and stir to loosen up the icing a bit.

The icing tips are clogging.

The combination of beating the meringue powder and water together, and sifting the powdered sugar, should prevent this. If a tip becomes clogged, remove the tip and push the clog through the tip with a toothpick.

The royal icing is too loose and runny for piping.

Stir in some sifted powdered sugar and stir with a silicone spatula. The icing can also be beaten again with a paddle attachment; add sifted powdered sugar and beat until stiff peaks form.

The royal icing has an off-taste.

I strongly encourage you to use a meringue powder from a bakery supply or kitchen shop. Meringue powder can vary in taste, so experiment and find which one you like best.

The colors are bleeding when I am making flat dots.

Dark colors dropped onto a light base are more likely to bleed. To prevent this, wait a few extra minutes before dropping on the dots. Using a high-quality gel paste food coloring also seems to help. If your dots do bleed a bit, you are most likely the only one who notices. Take a step back, take a deep breath, and remember, it's just a cookie.

Because these daisies are perfect for a variety of occasions, they're a great "go-to" project when you want to make cookies and can't decide on a design. Change up the colors any way you want and add them to another design for an instant cookie assortment.

you will need

Vanilla-Almond Sugar Cookies (page 22), daisy shape

Royal Icing (page 28), divided and tinted:
EGG YELLOW • WHITE

Disposable icing bag

Coupler

Icing tip: #3

Squeeze bottle

Toothpicks

DAISIES

1 Scoop some yellow icing into a bag and use a #3 tip to outline the daisy petals. Ⓐ

2 Thin the white icing for flooding (as described on page 16). Cover the icing with a damp dish towel and let it sit for several minutes. Gently stir with a silicone spatula and transfer the icing to a squeeze bottle.

3 Fill in the petals with the thinned white icing. Use a toothpick to guide icing to the edges and pop air bubbles. Ⓑ

4 Move the icing bag of yellow icing back and forth to fill in the center with yellow icing.

5 Let the cookies dry uncovered for 6 to 8 hours or overnight.

For me, bite-size cookies are the hardest to resist. And who can pass up a sparkly, sugary, heart-shaped cookie? I use sanding sugar here, but you can always use the larger grained sparkling sugar.

you will need

Vanilla-Almond Sugar Cookies (page 22), mini-heart shape

Royal Icing (page 28), divided and tinted:
RED • PINK • WHITE

Disposable icing bags (3)

Couplers, Icing tips: #2

Squeeze bottles (3)

Toothpicks, Meringue powder

Small paintbrush

Sanding sugar: red, pink, white

SPARKLING HEARTS

1 Scoop some of each icing color into the bags and attach #2 tips. Outline the cookies in each of the colors. Ⓐ

2 Squeeze leftover piping colors back into the original bowls, and thin all three icings for flooding (as described on page 16). Cover the icings with a damp dishtowel and let them sit for several minutes. Gently stir with a silicone spatula and transfer the icings to squeeze bottles as needed.

3 Fill in the hearts with the thinned icing. Use a toothpick to guide icing to the edges and pop air bubbles. Let the cookies dry uncovered for 6 to 8 hours or overnight. Ⓑ

4 Once the cookies are dry, mix $1/2$ teaspoon meringue powder with $1/2$ teaspoon water. Brush the cookies with the mixture and sprinkle on the sanding sugar (as described on page 19). Shake off the excess. The cookies will be dry and ready to package in 15 to 30 minutes.

SEASHELLS

These simple seashell cookies are the next best
thing to going to the beach. Come to think of
it—no sunburn, no jellyfish, no swimsuit anxiety—
they're better than the beach!

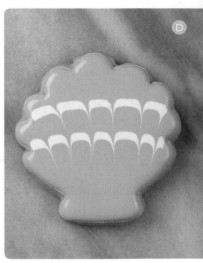

you will need

Vanilla-Almond Sugar Cookies
(page 22), seashell shape

Royal Icing (page 28), divided and
tinted:
TURQUOISE • WHITE

Disposable icing bag

Coupler

Icing tip: #2

Squeeze bottles (2)

Toothpicks

Variation
Meringue powder

Small paintbrush

White sanding sugar

1 Scoop some turquoise icing into the bag and use a #2 tip to outline the shell. (A)

2 Squeeze leftover turquoise icing back into the bowl, and thin
both the turquoise and the white icing for flooding (as described on
page 16). Cover the icings with a damp dishtowel and let them sit
for several minutes. Gently stir with a silicone spatula and transfer
the icings to squeeze bottles.

3 Working six cookies at a time, fill in the outlines with the thinned
turquoise icing. Use a toothpick to guide icing to the edges and pop
air bubbles. (B)

4 Starting with the first filled cookie, squeeze two horizontal
lines of thinned white icing across the cookie on top of the wet
turquoise icing. (C)
→ Drag a toothpick down through the icing several times to create a
marbled look (as described on page 18). (D)

5 Let the cookies dry uncovered for 6 to 8 hours or overnight.

Variation

If desired, cover the entire cookie in sanding sugar. Mix $1/2$ teaspoon
meringue powder with $1/2$ teaspoon water. Brush the cookies with
the mixture, using a small, clean paintbrush. Sprinkle on white sanding sugar (as described on page 19). Shake off the excess.

MERMAIDS

PAGE 34

I love that these mermaid cookies are totally customizable. Change the eye color, skin tone, and hair color to make them your own.

you will need

Vanilla-Almond Sugar Cookies (page 22), mermaid shape

Royal Icing (page 28), divided and tinted:
DEEP PINK OR EGG YELLOW • LIGHT COPPER OR WARM BROWN (SKIN TONE) • ORANGE OR BLACK • LEAF GREEN • CHOCOLATE BROWN • RED

Disposable icing bags (6)

Couplers

Icing tips: #2, #1

Squeeze bottles (4)

Toothpicks

1 Scoop some of the first four icing colors into bags and attach #2 tips.
→ Outline the shell-shaped bikini top in pink or yellow icing. A
→ Outline the head, shoulders, torso, and arms of the mermaids in skin tone icing. B
→ Outline the hair in orange or black icing. Scrape away any skin tone icing that ends up inside the hair outline. C
→ Outline the tail in green icing. D
→ Reserve some of each color (except the flesh tone) in the bags for piping details.

2 Still using just the first four colors, thin the remaining icing for flooding (as described on page 16). Cover the icings with a damp dishtowel and let them sit for several minutes. Gently stir with a silicone spatula and transfer the icings to squeeze bottles as needed.

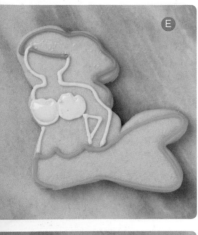

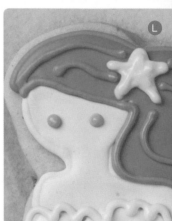

3 Fill in the outlines for the tops. Use a toothpick to guide icing to the edges and pop air bubbles. Do the same for the body, hair, and tail. Let the cookies dry for 1 hour. E F G H

4 Pipe on the following details:

→ Switch the #2 tip on the pink or yellow icing to a #1 tip. Pipe over the outline of the tops, and add detail piping in the middle. Pipe a star shape in the hair. I

→ Use a #1 tip with orange or black icing to add detail to the hair. J

→ Use a #2 tip with green icing to go back over the tail outline and add detail.

→ Use a #1 tip with black icing to add a belly button. K

→ Use a #1 tip with green or chocolate brown icing to pipe the eyes. L

→ Use a #1 tip with red icing to add the heart-shaped mouth. M

5 Let the cookies dry uncovered for 6 to 8 hours or overnight.

GIVE A HOOT

You might not know it, but owls are multitaskers.
Birthday party, woodland soirée, autumnal celebration,
graduation gift—owls are always a hit! I made boy and
girl owls here, but any color will do.

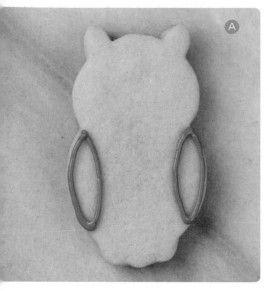
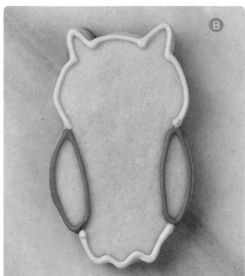
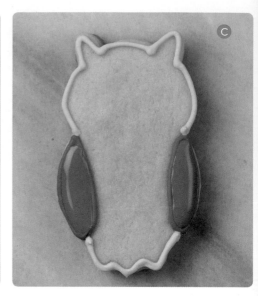

you will need

Vanilla-Almond Sugar Cookies (page 22), owl shape

Royal Icing (page 28), divided and tinted:
CHOCOLATE BROWN • DEEP PINK • SKY BLUE • WHITE • BLACK • ORANGE

Disposable icing bags (6)

Couplers

Icing tips: #2, #12, #3, #1

Squeeze bottles (3)

Toothpicks

Black fine-tipped food-coloring pen

1 Scoop some of the brown, pink, and blue icings into the bags and attach #2 tips.
→ Outline the wings in brown. Squeeze leftover brown icing back into the bowl. Ⓐ
→ Outline the bodies, some with pink and some with blue. Ⓑ
→ Reserve some of the pink and blue icing in the bags for piping details.

2 Thin the remaining brown, pink, and blue icings for flooding (as described on page 16). Cover them with a damp dishtowel and let them sit for several minutes. Gently stir with a silicone spatula and transfer icing to squeeze bottles as needed.

3 Fill in the wings with brown thinned icing, Ⓒ and the bodies in pink or blue. Use a toothpick to guide icing to the edges and pop air bubbles.

4 Because the eyes are a large piped detail, let the cookies dry for at least 1 hour to avoid disturbing the flood icing.

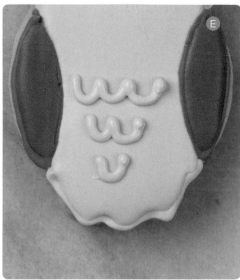

TIP *When piping details such as eyes and dots, stop squeezing the piping bag before lifting. If points are forming, thin the icing with a drop or two of water to loosen it. (I tend not to worry about this much.)*

5 Pipe large white eyes onto the owls, using a #12 round tip. Pipe black pupils directly on top of the freshly piped white icing, using a #3 tip. D

6 For the final touches:
→ Use a #1 tip with blue or pink icing to add the feather detail on the body. E
→ Use a #1 tip with orange icing to pipe a beak and toes. F

7 Let the cookies dry uncovered for 6 to 8 hours or overnight. Once the cookies are completely dry, use a black food-coloring pen to add the eyelashes on the girl owls. G

MUSHROOMS

I guarantee your kids will eat these mushrooms. These employ my favorite decorating technique: the flat dot. The flat dot = instant cute.

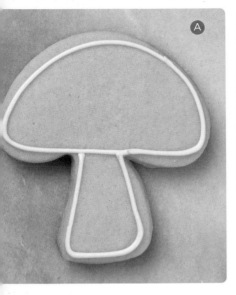
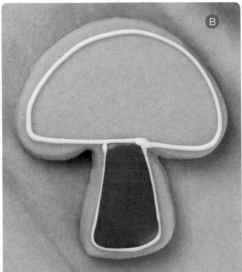

you will need

Vanilla-Almond Sugar Cookies (page 22), mushroom shape

Royal Icing (page 28), divided and tinted:
WHITE • CHOCOLATE BROWN • RED • SKY BLUE

Disposable icing bag

Coupler

Icing tip: #2

Squeeze bottles (4)

Toothpicks

1 Scoop some white icing into a bag and use a #2 tip to outline each mushroom shape. Squeeze the leftover white icing back into the bowl. Ⓐ

2 Thin all four icing colors for flooding (as described on page 16). Cover the icings with a damp dishtowel and let them sit for several minutes. Gently stir with a silicone spatula and transfer icing to squeeze bottles as needed.

3 Fill in the mushroom bottoms with thinned brown icing. Use a toothpick to guide icing to the edges and pop air bubbles. Ⓑ

4 Working six cookies at a time:
➜ Fill in the mushroom tops with the thinned red or blue icing, using a toothpick as before.
➜ On top of the wet red and blue icing, drop dots of the thinned white icing. (The flat dot technique is described on page 17). Ⓒ

5 Let the cookies dry uncovered for 6 to 8 hours or overnight.

DRAGONFLIES

Iridescent dragonfly wings are an excellent excuse to break
out the disco dust. Just be prepared to wear that disco dust
in your hair, on your arms, and across your face for the rest
of the day (don't say I didn't warn you).

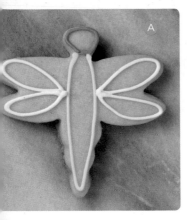

you will need

Vanilla-Almond Sugar Cookies (page 22), dragonfly shape

Royal Icing (page 28), divided and tinted:
ROYAL BLUE • ELECTRIC GREEN • WHITE • BLACK

Disposable icing bags (4)

Couplers

Icing tips: #2, #1

Squeeze bottles (3)

Toothpicks

Meringue powder

Rainbow disco dust

Small paintbrush

1 Scoop some of the blue, green, and white icings into the bags and attach #2 tips.
→ Outline the head of the dragonfly in blue icing.
→ Outline the body in green icing.
→ Outline the wings in white icing. Ⓐ
→ Reserve some of the blue and white icing in the bags for piping details.

2 Thin the remaining blue, green, and white icings for flooding (as described on page 16). Cover them with a damp dishtowel and let them sit for several minutes. Gently stir with a silicone spatula and transfer icing to squeeze bottles as needed.

3 Fill in each section with the same color as the outlines, using a toothpick to guide icing to the edges and pop air bubbles. Let the cookies dry for 30 minutes. Ⓑ

4 Pipe on the following details:
→ Use a #1 tip with blue icing to pipe small stripes across the body. Ⓒ
→ Use a #1 tip with white icing to add detail piping to the wings.
→ Use a #1 tip with black icing to add eyes to the face. Ⓓ

5 Let the cookies dry uncovered for 6 to 8 hours or overnight.

6 Once the cookies are dry, mix ¼ teaspoon meringue powder with ¼ teaspoon water. Sprinkle on the disco dust and shake off the excess. Use a dry paintbrush to brush away disco dust that is sticking to other parts of the cookie, if desired. (Details for applying disco dust are on page 20.)

TIGER & PANDA

Basic cookie cutter shapes, like circles and squares, lend themselves to myriad cookie designs. Here I used a circle to make simple panda and tiger faces.

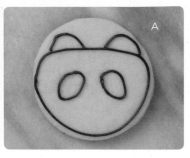 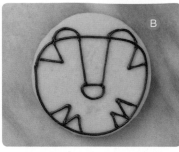  

  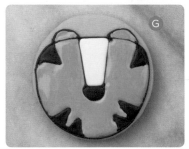 

you will need

Vanilla-Almond Sugar Cookies (page 22), circles

Royal Icing (page 28), divided and tinted:
BLACK • WHITE • ORANGE

Disposable icing bags (2)

Couplers

Icing tips: #2, #1

Squeeze bottles (3)

Toothpicks

Pink food-coloring pen

1 Scoop some black icing into a bag and use a #2 tip to outline the head and ears of the pandas and tigers. On the pandas, outline the eyes. On the tigers, outline some stripes. Save the black icing in the bag and reserve some white, as well, for piping details.

2 Thin the remaining black, white, and orange icings for flooding (as described on page 16). Cover the icings with a damp dishtowel and let them sit for several minutes. Gently stir with a silicone spatula and transfer icing to squeeze bottles as needed.

3 Fill in outlined areas with thinned icing as follows, using a toothpick to guide it to the edges and pop air bubbles:
→ Use black icing to fill in the panda eyes and ears, and the tiger stripes and nose.
→ Use white icing to fill in the panda face and the middle tiger stripe.
→ Use orange icing to fill in the tiger face.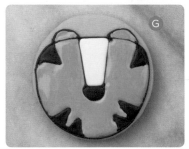

4 Let the cookies dry for 30 minutes.

5 Pipe on the following details:
→ Use a #2 tip with white icing to add detail to the panda eyes.
→ Use a #1 tip with black icing to add detail smiles to the panda  and tiger. Also, pipe eyes onto the tiger face.

6 Let the cookies dry uncovered for 6 to 8 hours or overnight. When they are completely dry, use a pink food-coloring pen to make a nose on each panda face.

CIRCUS TENTS

I can recall going to the circus only once in my life. I was six, and my dad treated me to a special father-daughter night out. In my mind, the circus tent looked exactly like this one.

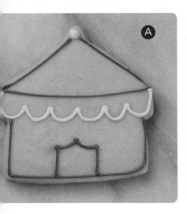
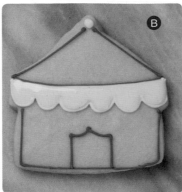

you will need

Vanilla-Almond Sugar Cookies (page 22), circus tent shape

Royal Icing (page 28), divided and tinted:
RED • EGG YELLOW • WHITE

Disposable icing bags (2)

Couplers

Icing tips: #2

Squeeze bottles (3)

Toothpicks

1 Scoop some of the red and yellow icings into bags and attach #2 tips.
➔ With red icing, pipe a line for the bottom of the roof.
➔ With yellow icing, pipe the scalloped awning right under the red roof line, then pipe a circle at the top of the tent.
➔ Going back to the red icing, add the remainder of the tent outline and outline the door opening. Ⓐ
➔ Reserve some of both colors in the bags for later piping details.

2 Thin the remaining red, yellow, and white icings for flooding (as described on page 16). Cover the icings with a damp dishtowel and let them sit for several minutes. Gently stir with a silicone spatula and transfer icing to squeeze bottles as needed.

3 Fill in the scalloped awning with thinned yellow icing, using a toothpick to guide icing to the edges and pop air bubbles. Ⓑ

4 Working six cookies at a time:
➔ Fill in the tent with thinned white icing.
➔ Starting with the first cookie filled, go back over the wet white icing with thinned red icing to add curved stripes on the roof and straight stripes down the front. Ⓒ
➔ Fill the door shape with thinned red icing.

5 Let the cookies dry for 30 minutes.

6 Pipe on the following details:
➔ Use a #2 tip with yellow icing to outline the awning. Ⓓ
➔ Use a #2 tip with red icing to outline the door.

7 Let the cookies dry uncovered for 6 to 8 hours or overnight.

CIRCUS ELEPHANTS

You'll be combining two cookie shapes here to make a new one. Don't worry—it's easy!

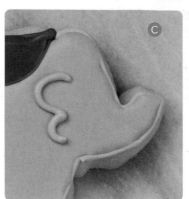

you will need

Star Embellishment

Royal Icing (page 28), tinted:
EGG YELLOW

Star template from page 156

Waxed paper

Disposable icing bag

Coupler

Icing tip: #2 or #3

Squeeze bottle

Cookies

Vanilla-Almond Sugar Cookie dough (page 22)

Elephant and candy corn cookie cutters

Royal Icing (page 28), divided and tinted:
RED • GRAY (MADE USING BLACK) •
ROYAL BLUE • BLACK •
EGG YELLOW

Disposable icing bags (5)

Couplers

Icing tips: #2, #3, #1

Squeeze bottles (2), Toothpicks

1 At least a day (and up to 2 weeks) before making the cookies, make the star embellishments. Using the method described on page 18, pipe star shapes in yellow icing onto waxed paper, using a #2 or #3 tip, then thin the icing and fill the shapes (see below). Be sure to make more than you need, because they are fragile. Let the stars dry overnight, carefully remove them from the waxed paper, and store in an airtight container until ready to use.

2 To make the custom cookie shape, use cookie cutters to cut elephants and candy corns from cookie dough. To make a pedestal, trim off the top of the candy corn shapes with a bench scraper or paring knife. Gently squeeze the elephant legs together to fit the top of the pedestal. Place the shapes together on a cookie sheet and freeze for at least 10 minutes before baking. Bake and cool completely as usual.

3 Scoop some of the red and gray icings into bags and attach #2 tips.
→ With red icing, outline the pedestal and the blanket on the elephant.
→ With gray icing, outline the elephant body and pipe the tail. Reserve some gray icing in the bag for piping details. Ⓐ

4 Thin the remaining red and gray icings for flooding (as described on page 16). Cover the icings with a damp dishtowel and let them sit for several minutes. Gently stir with a silicone spatula and transfer icing to squeeze bottles as needed.

5 Fill in the elephant with thinned gray icing, and fill in the pedestal and blanket with thinned red icing. Use a toothpick to guide icing to the edges and pop air bubbles. Let the icing dry for about 30 minutes.

6 Gently place the star on the red icing. (Details on adding embellishments are on page 19.)

7 Pipe on the following details:
→ Use a #3 tip with blue icing to add lines on the top and bottom of the pedestal. Ⓑ
→ Use a #2 tip with gray icing to add an ear to the elephant. Ⓒ
→ Use a #1 tip with black icing to add an eye. Ⓓ
→ Use a #1 tip with yellow icing to add dots to the blanket edge and on the blue lines.

8 Let the cookies dry uncovered for 6 to 8 hours or overnight.

MAGIC RABBITS

It doesn't take much magic to make these rabbit-out-of-a-hat cookies. What's the trick? Putting together two cookie shapes you probably already have in your arsenal.

 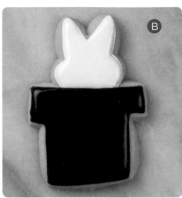 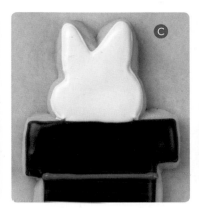 

you will need

Vanilla-Almond Sugar Cookie dough (page 22)

Bunny and square cookie cutters

Royal Icing (page 28), divided and tinted:
BLACK • WHITE • RED • EGG YELLOW

Disposable icing bags (4)

Couplers

Icing tips: #2, #3, #1

Squeeze bottles (2)

Toothpicks

Pink food-coloring pen

1 To make the custom cookie shape, use cookie cutters to cut bunnies and squares from cookie dough. Using a bench scraper or paring knife, trim off the bunny's head, and trim edges off the sides of the square to make a hat. Place the shapes together on a cookie sheet and freeze for at least 10 minutes before baking. Bake and cool completely as usual.

2 Scoop some black and white icings into bags and attach #2 tips.
→ Outline the hat in black icing. Reserve some black icing in the bag for piping details.
→ Outline the rabbit shape in white icing. Ⓐ

3 Thin the remaining black and white icings for flooding (as described on page 16). Cover the icings with a damp dishtowel and let them sit for several minutes. Gently stir with a silicone spatula and transfer icing to squeeze bottles as needed.

4 Fill in the hat with thinned black icing, and fill in the rabbit with thinned white icing. Use a toothpick to guide icing to the edges and pop air bubbles. Let the cookies dry for 30 minutes. Ⓑ

5 Pipe on the following details:
→ Use a #3 tip with red icing to add a line on the hat. Ⓒ
→ Use a #1 tip with yellow icing to add a flower to the hat.
→ Use a #2 tip with black icing to add eyes on the bunny face.
→ Use a #1 tip with red icing to add a dot to the center of the flower. Ⓓ

6 Let the cookies dry uncovered for 6 to 8 hours or overnight. When the cookies are completely dry, use a pink food-coloring pen to make a nose on the rabbit face.

MONOGRAMMED HOUSES

you will need

Monogram Embellishment
Royal Icing (page 28), divided and tinted:
VIOLET • ELECTRIC PINK

Waxed paper

Disposable icing bags (2)

Coupler, Icing tip: #2 or #3

Cookies
Vanilla-Almond Sugar Cookies (page 22), house shape

Royal Icing (page 28), divided and tinted:
VIOLET • ELECTRIC PINK • IVORY • LEMON YELLOW

Disposable icing bags (2)

Couplers, Icing tip: #3

Squeeze bottles (2)

Toothpicks

1 At least a day (and up to 2 weeks) before making the cookies, make the monogram embellishments. Using the method described on page 18, pipe monograms in violet and electric pink onto waxed paper using a #3 tip. Be sure to make more than you need, because they are fragile. Let the monograms dry overnight, carefully remove them from the waxed paper, and store in an airtight container until ready to use.

2 Scoop some violet and electric pink icings into bags and use #3 tips to outline the houses, some in each color. Ⓐ

3 Thin the ivory and yellow icings for flooding (as described on page 16). Cover the icings with a damp dishtowel and let them sit for several minutes. Gently stir with a silicone spatula and transfer icing to squeeze bottles as needed.

4 Fill in the cookies with the thinned icing, using ivory for the cookies outlined in violet and yellow for the cookies outlined in pink. Use a toothpick to guide icing to the edges and pop air bubbles. Let the icing dry for about 30 minutes. Ⓑ

5 Gently place the monograms on the icing. (Details on adding embellishments are on page 19.) Let the cookies dry uncovered for 6 to 8 hours or overnight.

Variation
If desired, thin the colors used for the outline and the monogram and add dots to the houses, using the flat dot method (as described on page 17).

I'll be honest: this pigeon-toed girl was never a fan of ballet class. But the shoes, oh, now that's another story.

BALLET SLIPPERS

you will need

Vanilla-Almond Sugar Cookies (page 22), ballet slipper shapes

Royal Icing (page 28), divided and tinted:
ROSE PINK • WHITE

Disposable icing bags (2)

Couplers

Icing tips: #2

Squeeze bottles (2)

Toothpicks

1 Scoop some of both icings into bags and attach #2 tips.
→ Outline the slipper and ribbon with rose icing. Scrape off any outlines where two overlap, using a toothpick. Reserve some rose icing in the bag for piping details.
→ Outline the open areas with white icing. Ⓐ

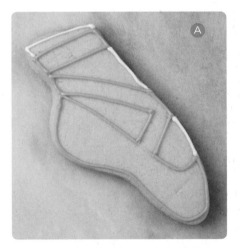

2 Thin the remaining rose and white icings for flooding (as described on page 16). Cover the icings with a damp dishtowel and let them sit for several minutes. Gently stir with a silicone spatula and transfer icing to squeeze bottles as needed.

3 Fill in the shoe and ribbon with thinned rose icing. Ⓑ Fill in the remaining areas with thinned white icing. Use a toothpick to guide icing to the edges and pop air bubbles.

4 Use the #2 tip with rose icing to go back over the outline of the shoe and the ribbon.

5 Let the cookies dry uncovered for 6 to 8 hours or overnight.

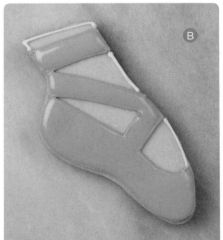

HEART BOTS

As the mom of a boy, I've noticed they get the short end of the stick when it comes to Valentine's Day. Everything is pink and girly, but boys deserve to celebrate, too! These robots are just the ticket—cool, boyish, but still filled with love.

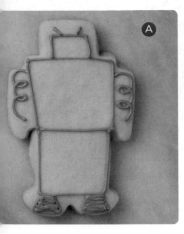
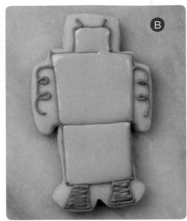

you will need

Vanilla-Almond Sugar Cookies (page 22), robot shape

Royal Icing (page 28), divided and tinted:
DARK GRAY (MADE USING BLACK) •
LIGHT GRAY (MADE USING BLACK) •
RED • WHITE • BLACK

Disposable icing bags (4)

Couplers

Icing tips: #2, #1

Squeeze bottles (2)

Toothpicks

1 Scoop dark gray icing into a bag and attach a #2 tip. Outline the robot body parts: arms, antennae, and shoes. Reserve this bag for piping details. Ⓐ

2 Thin the light gray icing for flooding (as described on page 16). Cover the icing with a damp dishtowel and let it sit for several minutes. Gently stir with a silicone spatula and transfer the icing to a squeeze bottle.

3 Fill in the robot outline, using a toothpick to guide icing to the edges and pop air bubbles. Let the cookies dry for at least 1 hour. Ⓑ

4 Scoop some of the red icing into a bag and attach a #2 tip.
→ Outline a heart on the robot with red icing.
→ Add hearts to the antennae and form claws for the hands. Ⓒ
→ Reserve this bag for later piping details.

5 Thin the remaining red icing for flooding (as described on page 16). Cover and let sit, as before, then stir and transfer the icing to a squeeze bottle. Fill in the heart with red icing.

6 Pipe on the following details:
→ Use a #1 tip with white icing to make the eyeballs, squeezing a little longer to make a large dot.
→ Directly on top of the white icing, use a #1 tip with black icing to add pupils to the eyes.
→ Use a #1 tip with red icing to pipe a smile on the robot. Ⓓ
→ Go back over the outline of the robot with a #2 tip and dark gray icing. Add dots along the edges of the chest and knees (for bolts), and add ears.

7 Let the cookies dry uncovered for 6 to 8 hours or overnight.

PHOTO LOCKETS

Inspired by vintage lockets, these cookies use a black-and-white photo printed on frosting sheets for a nostalgic look. If you don't have an icing printer, ask your local bakery supply or grocery store bakery to print them for you.

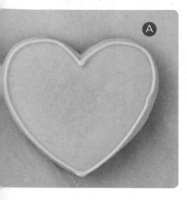
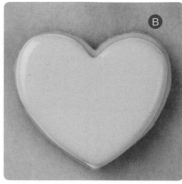

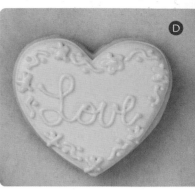

you will need

Vanilla-Almond Sugar Cookies (page 22), heart shape

Heart-shaped cookie cutter (same size as the cookies)

Edible images (details on page 20)

Royal Icing (page 28), tinted: GOLD

Disposable icing bag

Coupler

Icing tips: #2, #1

Squeeze bottle

Toothpicks

Gold luster dust

Vodka

Small paintbrush

1 Using the heart-shaped cookie cutter as a reference, cut the edible frosting sheets into heart shapes that are a bit smaller than the cutter. Leave the backing intact and set aside.

2 Scoop some gold icing into a bag and use a #2 tip to outline the hearts. Reserve some gold icing in the bag for piping details. Ⓐ

3 Thin the remaining gold icing for flooding (as described on page 16). Cover the icing with a damp dishtowel and let it sit for several minutes. Gently stir with a silicone spatula and transfer the icing to a squeeze bottle.

4 Fill in the hearts with the thinned icing. Use a toothpick to guide icing to the edges and pop air bubbles. Ⓑ

5 Remove the backing from the edible images and place them on half of the cookies, directly on top of the wet icing. Ⓒ

6 Pipe on the following:
→ Switch to a #1 tip on the gold bag, and add detail to the remaining plain hearts. Pipe the word "Love" in the center and draw a border along the edges, or use a design of your own. Ⓓ

7 Let the cookies dry uncovered for 6 to 8 hours or overnight.

8 Mix together ¼ teaspoon gold luster dust with several drops of vodka. Brush the mixture onto the plain hearts and the border of the edible image hearts, using a small, clean paintbrush. (Details on applying luster dust are on page 20.) Because cookies with edible images can take longer to dry, allow at least 24 hours for drying.

VALENTINE HEARTS

Pink, polka dots, and flowers ... cookies don't get much more girly than these. Placed in an individual bag and tied with a ribbon, even one makes a sweet little gift. Send them to school with the kids, take a few to the neighbors, and leave one for the mail carrier. Spread the love this Valentine's Day.

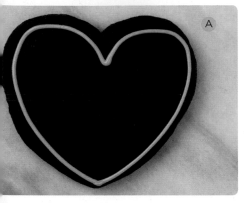
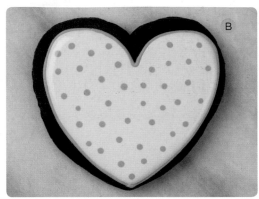

you will need

Chocolate-Hazelnut Cookies (page 24), heart shape

Royal Icing (page 28), divided and tinted:
DEEP PINK • SOFT PINK • LEMON YELLOW • LEAF GREEN

Disposable icing bags (3)

Couplers

Icing tips: #3, #15 or #16 star, #2, #1

Squeeze bottles (2)

Toothpicks

1 Scoop some deep pink icing into a bag and use a #3 tip to outline the hearts. Reserve some icing in the bag for piping details. Ⓐ

2 Thin the remaining deep and soft pink icings for flooding (as described on page 16). Cover the icings with a damp dishtowel and let them sit for several minutes. Gently stir with a silicone spatula and transfer the icings to squeeze bottles.

3 Working six cookies at a time, fill in the hearts with the soft pink icing. Use a toothpick to guide icing to the edges and pop air bubbles. On top of the wet icing, drop small dots using the thinned deep pink icing. (The flat dot technique is described on page 17.) Let the cookies dry for 1 hour. Ⓑ

4 Pipe on the following details:
→ Use a #15 or #16 star tip with dark pink icing to pipe flowers in a cluster on the top side of the cookies.
→ Use a #2 tip with yellow icing to pipe dots beside the flowers.
→ Use a #1 tip with dark pink icing to add swirls on top of the yellow dots.
→ Use a #1 tip with green icing to pipe leaves around the flowers. Ⓒ

TIP *Piping flowers with a star tip calls for a stiff icing. Test the icing by piping flowers onto a plate or paper towel first. If the flowers don't hold their shape, stir in sifted powdered sugar until the icing becomes stiff again.*

5 Let the cookies dry uncovered for 6 to 8 hours or overnight.

Variation
Instead of adding the flowers in a cluster on the top side of the cookies, spread the flowers along the top or scatter them across the cookies.

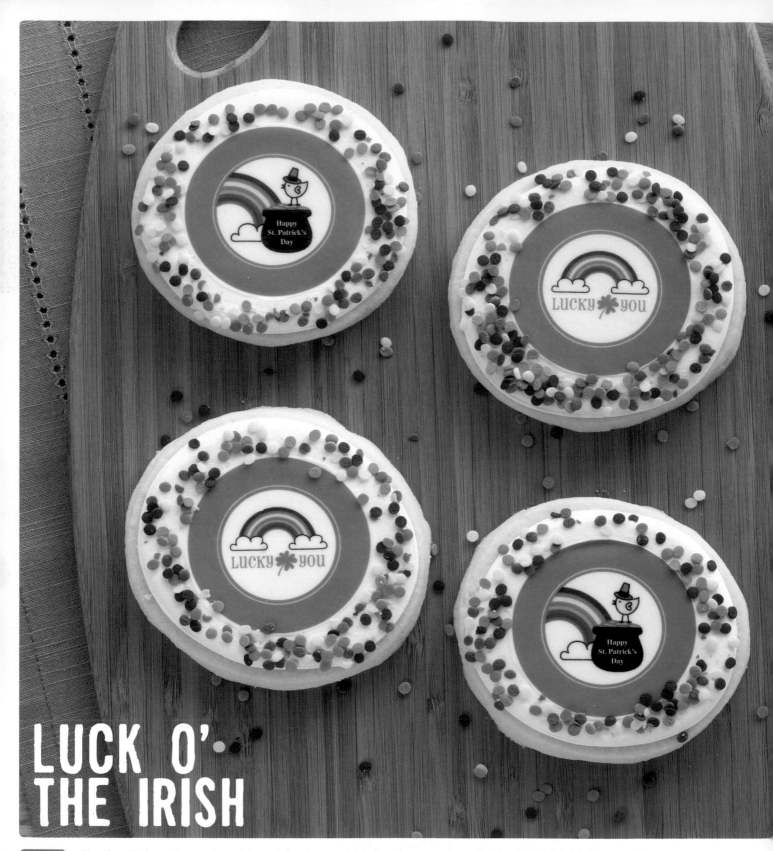

LUCK O'
THE IRISH

Our family has always loved to celebrate our Irish heritage, so I can't let a St. Patrick's Day go by
without cookies! The edible images were created by my friend, Amy, of www.livinglocurto.com
and are included for you to use on page 157. If you don't have an icing printer, ask your local
bakery supply or grocery store bakery to print them for you.

you will need

Vanilla-Almond Sugar Cookies (page 22), circles

Edible images (details on page 20)

Royal Icing (page 28), tinted: **WHITE**

Disposable icing bag

Coupler

Icing tip: #2

Squeeze bottles

Toothpicks

Meringue powder

Small paintbrush

Rainbow sprinkles

1 Cut the edible images, leaving the backing intact and set aside.

Note: I printed these edible images with a 2-inch diameter, and my cookies were cut with a 3-inch cookie cutter.

2 Scoop some white icing into a bag and use a #2 tip to outline the circles. Return the leftover white icing to the bowl. Ⓐ

3 Thin the remaining white icing for flooding (as described on page 16). Cover the icing with a damp dishtowel and let it sit for several minutes. Gently stir with a silicone spatula and transfer the icing to a squeeze bottle.

4 Fill in the circle with the thinned white icing. Use a toothpick to guide icing to the edges and pop air bubbles. Ⓑ

5 Remove the backing from the edible images and place them on the cookies, directly on top of the wet icing. Ⓒ Ⓓ

6 Let the cookies dry 6 to 8 hours or overnight.

7 Mix together 1/4 teaspoon meringue powder with 1/4 teaspoon water. Brush the border of the cookies (not covered by the edible image) with the mixture and sprinkle on the rainbow sprinkles (as described on page 19). Shake off the excess.

Because cookies with edible images can take longer to dry, allow at least 24 hours for drying.

BRIDAL SHOWER MONOGRAMS

Elegant and refined or fun and funky—take your pick. Monogrammed cookies for a bridal shower can fit any shower décor.

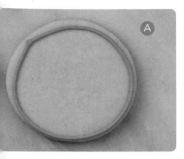

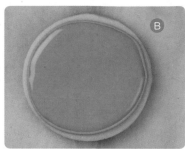

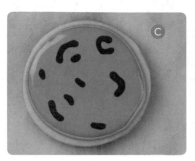

you will need

1 At least a day (and up to 2 weeks) before making the cookies, make the monogram embellishments. Using the method described on page 18, pipe the monograms in ivory or electric pink onto waxed paper, using a #3 tip. Use any font you like, or try the one on page 157. Be sure to make more than you need, because they are fragile. Let the monograms dry overnight, carefully remove them from the waxed paper, and store in an airtight container until ready to use. Save any leftover icing for piping the cookies.

2 Scoop some ivory and electric pink icings into bags and attach #3 tips.
→ Outline the circles in ivory (for elegant) or electric pink (for leopard). Ⓐ

3 *For the elegant cookies:* Thin the turquoise icing for flooding (as described on page 16). Cover the icing with a damp dishtowel and let it sit for several minutes. Gently stir with a silicone spatula and transfer the icing to a squeeze bottle. Fill in the cookies with the thinned icing, using a toothpick to guide icing to the edges and pop air bubbles.

4 *For the leopard print cookies:* Thin the ivory, warm brown, and black icings for flooding as described in step 3.
→ Working six cookies at a time, fill in the cookies with the thinned brown icing. Use a toothpick to guide icing to the edges and pop air bubbles. Ⓑ
→ Starting with the first filled cookie, pipe uneven and broken C shapes in thinned black icing on top of the wet brown icing. Ⓒ
→ Drop the thinned ivory icing into the center of the C shapes to create a leopard pattern. Ⓓ

5 Let the icing dry for about 30 minutes, then gently place the monograms on top. (Details on adding embellishments are on page 19.)

6 Let the cookies dry uncovered for 6 to 8 hours or overnight.

WEDDING DRESSES

It might be because of cookies that I can't fit into my actual wedding dress anymore. I'm okay with that.

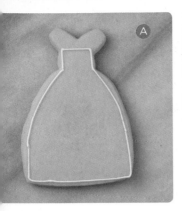

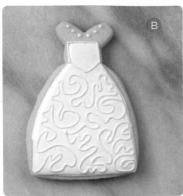

you will need

Vanilla-Almond Sugar Cookies (page 22), dress shape

Royal Icing (page 28), divided and tinted:
WHITE • GRAY (MADE USING BLACK)

Disposable icing bags (2)

Couplers

Icing tips: #2

Squeeze bottles (2)

Toothpicks

Meringue powder

Small paintbrushes (2)

Silver sanding sugar

Pearl luster dust

For the All-White Dress

1 Scoop some white icing into a bag and use a #2 tip to outline the dress. Reserve some icing in the bag for piping details. Ⓐ

2 Thin the remaining white icing for flooding (as described on page 16). Cover the icing with a damp dishtowel and let it sit for several minutes. Gently stir with a silicone spatula and transfer the icing to a squeeze bottle.

3 Fill in the dress with thinned white icing. Use a toothpick to guide icing to the edges and pop air bubbles. Let the cookies dry for at least 30 minutes.

4 Use the same piping bag to outline the top of the dress and to add a necklace and swirls on the skirt. Ⓑ

5 Let the cookies dry uncovered for 6 to 8 hours or overnight.

For the White & Silver Dress

1 Scoop some white and gray icings into bags and attach #2 tips.
➜ Outline the waist and bottom trim of the dress in gray.
➜ Outline the remainder of the dress in white. Ⓒ

2 Return the icings to the bowls and thin them for flooding (as described on page 16). Cover them with a damp dishtowel and let them sit for several minutes. Gently stir with a silicone spatula and transfer icing to squeeze bottles as needed.

3 Fill in the waist and trim with thinned gray icing. Fill in the remainder of the dress with thinned white icing. Use a toothpick to guide icing to the edges and pop air bubbles. Ⓓ

4 Let the cookies dry uncovered for 6 to 8 hours or overnight.

5 Mix together ¼ teaspoon meringue powder with ¼ teaspoon water. Brush the gray areas of the cookies with the mixture and sprinkle on the silver sanding sugar (as described on page 19). Shake off the excess.

6 To add shimmer to the dresses, brush dry pearl luster dust onto the white areas, using a small, clean paintbrush. (Details on applying luster dust are on page 20.)

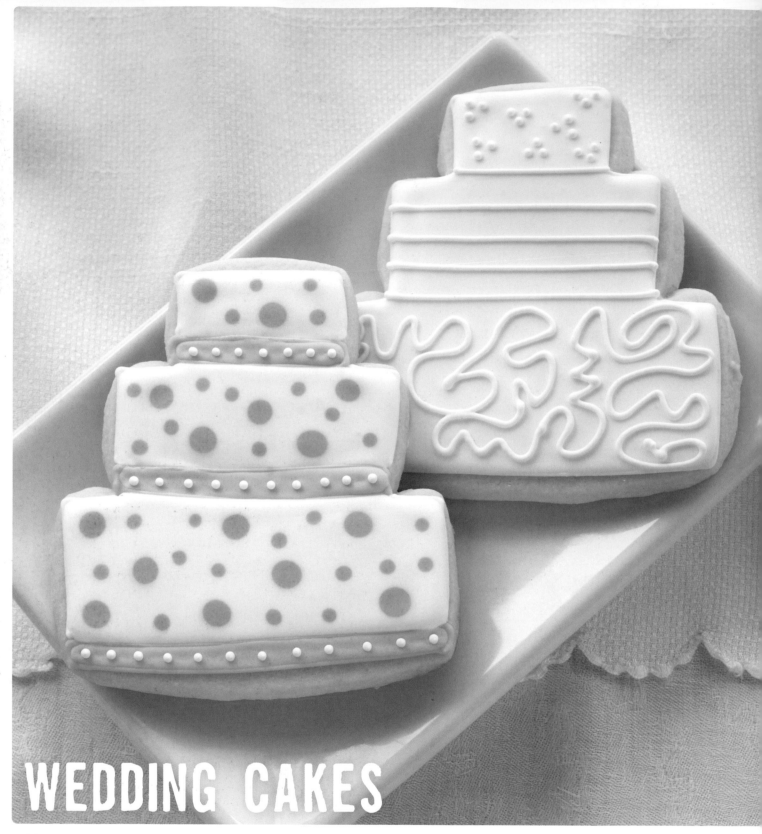

WEDDING CAKES

Let's face it: one of the best parts of getting married is picking out the cake. These cookie cakes are perfect for so many wedding festivities. Make them for rehearsal dinners, bridal showers, hostess gifts, out-of-town guests, or bridesmaids' presents. They are sure to be a hit.

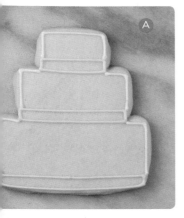 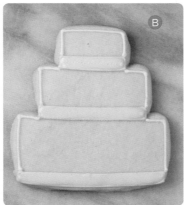  

you will need

Vanilla-Almond Sugar Cookies
(page 22), tiered cake shape

Royal Icing (page 28), divided
and tinted:
GREEN (AVOCADO MIXED WITH
LEAF GREEN) • WHITE • DEEP PINK

Disposable icing bags (2)

Couplers

Icing tips: #2, #1

Squeeze bottles (3)

Toothpicks

1 Scoop some green and white icings into bags and attach
#2 tips.
→ Outline the bottom of each tier with green icing.
→ Outline the remainder of the cake with white icing. Ⓐ

2 Thin the remaining green, white, and pink icings for flooding
(as described on page 16). Cover the icings with a damp dishtowel
and let them sit for several minutes. Gently stir with a silicone
spatula and transfer icing to squeeze bottles as needed.

3 Fill in the bottom of each tier with thinned green icing, using a
toothpick to guide icing to the edges and pop air bubbles. Ⓑ

4 Working six cookies at a time, fill in the remainder of the cakes
with the thinned white icing. Ⓒ On top of the wet icing, drop
small and large dots of thinned pink icing. (The flat dot technique
is described on page 17.) Ⓓ

5 Use a #1 tip with white to add detail dots to the green strip.

6 Let the cookies dry uncovered for 6 to 8 hours or overnight.

Variation
For an all-white cookie, outline and flood the cookie with white
icing. Use a #2 tip to cover the cookies in dots and swirls.

CHERRY BLOSSOMS

If there are no cherry trees
where you live, do what I
do: play make-believe
with cookies.

you will need

Vanilla-Almond Sugar Cookies (page 22), scalloped or plain squares

Royal Icing (page 28), divided and tinted:

DEEP PINK • SOFT PINK • CHOCOLATE BROWN • EGG YELLOW

Disposable icing bags (4)

Couplers

Icing tips: #2, #4, #1

Squeeze bottles (2)

Toothpicks

1 Scoop some deep pink icing into a bag and use a #2 tip to outline the squares. **A**

2 Return the deep pink icing to the bowl and thin it for flooding (as described on page 16). Cover the icing with a damp dishtowel and let it sit for several minutes. Gently stir with a silicone spatula and transfer the icing to a squeeze bottle.

3 Fill in the pink outline with the thinned icing, using a toothpick to guide icing to the edges and pop air bubbles. Allow the cookies to dry for at least 1 hour.

4 Scoop some soft pink icing into a bag, attach a #2 tip, and outline the three flowers on each square. Reserve some icing in the bag for later piping details. **B**

5 Thin the remaining soft pink icing for flooding, and prepare as before. Fill in each flower with soft pink icing.

6 Pipe on the following details:
➡ Use a #4 tip with brown icing to connect the flowers with branches. **C**
➡ Use a #2 tip with soft pink icing to pipe a few dots (flower buds) along the branches. **D**
➡ Use a #1 tip with yellow icing to add dots to the centers of the flowers.

7 Let the cookies dry uncovered for 6 to 8 hours or overnight.

COTTONTAIL CUTIES

I cannot resist those adorable little nonpareil cottontails, and they couldn't be simpler to make.

 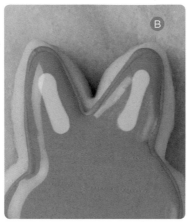 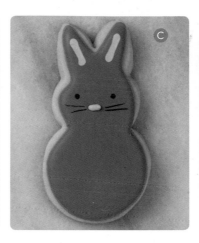 

you will need

Vanilla-Almond Sugar Cookies (page 22), bunny shape

Royal Icing (page 28), divided and tinted:
CHOCOLATE BROWN • DEEP PINK • WHITE

Disposable icing bags (3)

Couplers

Icing tips: #2, #1

Squeeze bottles (3)

Toothpicks

Black fine-tip food-coloring pen

Meringue powder

Small paintbrush

White nonpareils

1 Scoop some brown icing into a bag and use a #2 tip to outline the bunnies. Return the leftover brown icing to the bowl. Ⓐ

2 Reserve some of the pink icing for later piping details, then thin the remaining brown and pink icings for flooding (as described on page 16). Cover the icings with a damp dishtowel and let them sit for several minutes. Gently stir with a silicone spatula and transfer the icing to squeeze bottles.

3 Fill in the outline of all of the bunnies with thinned brown icing, using a toothpick to guide icing to the edges and pop air bubbles.

4 For the front view of the bunnies, add thinned pink icing for the ears on top of the wet brown icing. Ⓑ

5 For the back view of the bunnies, allow the cookies to dry for at least 1 hour. Then, use a #2 tip with white icing to outline each cottontail. Thin the remaining white icing for flooding as before and use it to fill in the cotton tail.

6 For the front view, use a #2 tip with pink icing to pipe a nose.

7 Let the cookies dry uncovered for 6 to 8 hours or overnight.

8 On the front-view bunnies, add whiskers and eyes with the fine-tip black food-coloring pen. Ⓒ

9 To finish the tail, mix together ¼ teaspoon meringue powder with ¼ teaspoon water. Brush the mixture onto the cottontails with a small paintbrush. Sprinkle on the nonpareils and shake off the excess. Ⓓ (Details for working with add-ons are on page 19.)

EASTER EGGS

Individually bagged and tied with a crisp, grosgrain ribbon, these cookies make a pretty addition to any Easter basket. And because Easter candy seems to revolve around chocolate, let's stick to the chocolate theme, shall we?

  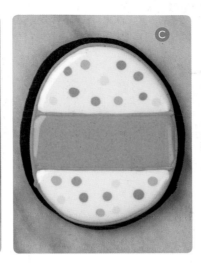 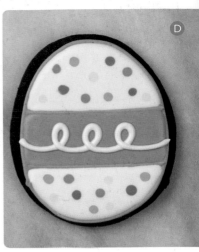

you will need

Chocolate-Hazelnut Cookies (page 24), egg shape

Royal Icing (page 28), divided and tinted:
ELECTRIC PINK • WHITE • EGG YELLOW • LEAF GREEN • PURPLE

Disposable icing bags (2)

Couplers

Icing tips: #3

Squeeze bottles (5)

Toothpicks

Meringue powder

Small paintbrush

White sanding sugar

1 Scoop some pink icing into a bag and attach a #3 tip. Outline the eggs, piping two horizontal lines to section off a top, middle, and bottom. Ⓐ

2 Reserve some piping-consistency white icing, then thin the yellow, green, purple, and remaining pink and white icings for flooding (as described on page 16). Cover the icings with a damp dishtowel and let them sit for several minutes. Gently stir with a silicone spatula and transfer the icings to squeeze bottles.

3 Working six cookies at a time, fill the top and bottom of the eggs with thinned white icing. Use a toothpick to guide icing to the edges and pop air bubbles. On top of the wet icing, drop small dots, using thinned icing in all of the colors. (The flat dot technique is described on page 17.) Ⓑ

4 Fill the center section of the eggs with thinned pink icing, using a toothpick as before. Let the cookies dry for 1 hour. Ⓒ

5 Use a #3 tip with white icing to pipe loops across the pink section. Let the cookies dry uncovered for 6 to 8 hours or overnight. Ⓓ

6 Mix together ¼ teaspoon meringue powder with ¼ teaspoon water. Brush the mixture on the loops, and sprinkle on the sanding sugar (as described on page 19). Shake off the excess. The cookies will be dry and ready to package in 15 to 30 minutes.

PERSONALIZED POSIES

These large posies might be my favorite way to decorate a girly cookie. I first made them for my friend Terri's birthday a few years ago, and I've been obsessed ever since. Here they make sweet baby shower favors.

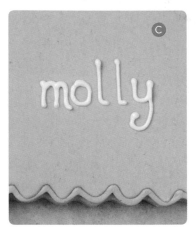

you will need

Vanilla-Almond Sugar Cookies
(page 22), scalloped squares

Royal Icing (page 28), divided
and tinted:
LEAF GREEN • DEEP PINK • WHITE •
SOFT PINK

Disposable icing bags (4)

Couplers

Icing tips: #3, #1, #7

Squeeze bottle

Toothpicks

1 Scoop some green icing into a bag and use a #3 tip to outline the cookie squares. Ⓐ

2 Reserve some of the deep pink icing, then thin the rest of it for flooding (as described on page 16). Cover the icing with a damp dishtowel and let it sit for several minutes. Gently stir with a silicone spatula and transfer the icing to a squeeze bottle.

3 Fill the squares with thinned deep pink icing. Use a toothpick to guide icing to the edges and pop air bubbles. Allow the cookies to dry for at least 1 hour. Ⓑ

4 Use a #1 tip with white icing to personalize the cookies. To help with centering, start with the middle letter and pipe the remainder of the letters out from the center. Ⓒ

5 Use a #7 tip with soft pink icing to pipe on the posies (flowers). If the icing is very stiff, add a drop or two of water to the icing before piping. This will help prevent large points in the center of the flowers. Ⓓ

6 Pipe on the following details:
→ Use a #1 tip with deep pink icing to make curlicues on top of the large posies.
→ Use a #1 tip with green icing to add leaves.

7 Let the cookies dry uncovered for 6 to 8 hours or overnight.

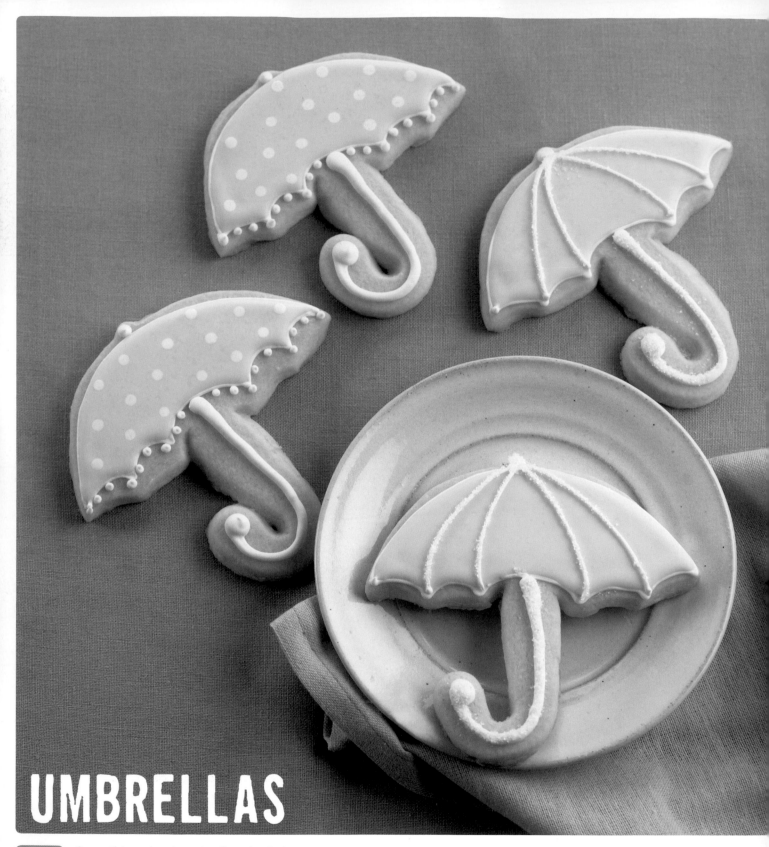

UMBRELLAS

Something about umbrellas at a baby
"shower" is so charming and nostalgic.
Serve the cookies during the party, or
package and give them as favors.

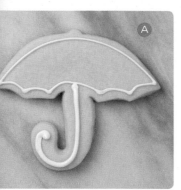

you will need

Vanilla-Almond Sugar Cookies (page 22), umbrella shape

Royal Icing (page 28), divided and tinted:
WHITE • LEMON YELLOW

Disposable icing bag

Couplers

Icing tips: #2, #4, #1

Squeeze bottles (2)

Toothpicks

Variation

Meringue powder

Small paintbrush

White sanding sugar

1 Scoop some white icing into a bag and attach a #2 tip.
→ Outline the tops of the umbrellas.
→ Switch to a #4 tip to pipe the handle of the umbrella. Ⓐ
→ Reserve some white icing in the bag for piping details.

2 Thin the remaining white and yellow icings for flooding (as described on page 16). Cover the icings with a damp dishtowel and let them sit for several minutes. Gently stir with a silicone spatula and transfer the icings to squeeze bottles as needed.

3 Working six cookies at a time, fill in the umbrella tops with the thinned yellow icing. Use a toothpick to guide icing to the edges and pop air bubbles. On top of the wet icing, drop dots of thinned white icing. (The flat dot technique is described on page 17.) Ⓑ

4 Use a #1 tip with white icing to add dots along the bottom border of the umbrellas. Ⓒ

Variation
Instead of white dots, use a #2 tip with white icing to pipe detail lines from the top center to the points along the bottom. Ⓓ Let the cookies dry overnight. Once dry, mix ¼ teaspoon water with ¼ teaspoon meringue powder. Apply the mixture to the white piping and umbrella handle with a small paintbrush. Sprinkle with white sanding sugar and shake off the excess (as described on page 19).

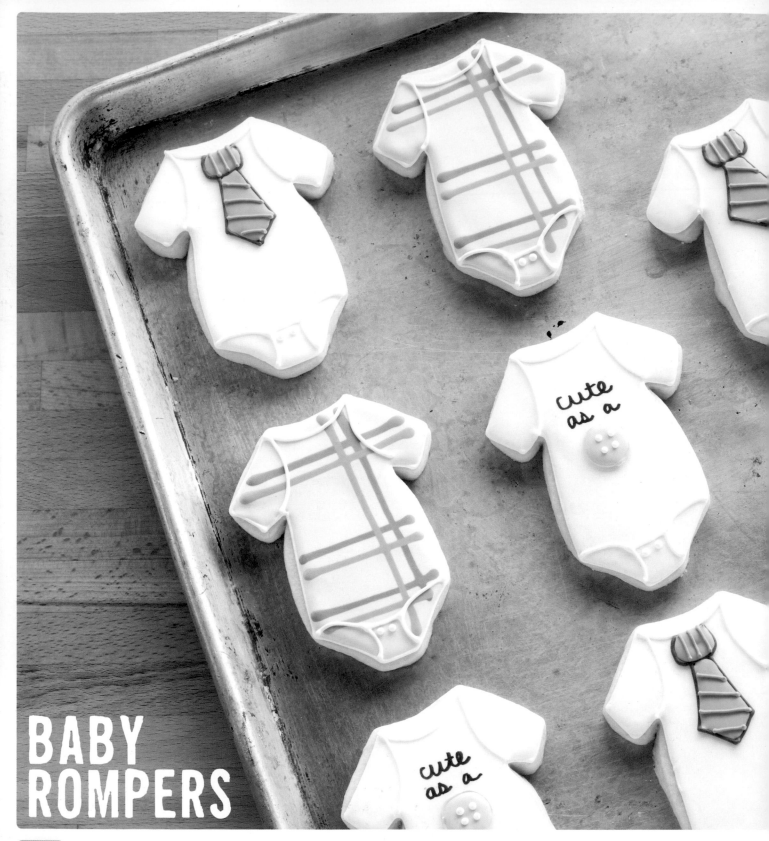

BABY ROMPERS

Whoever invented these little one-piece baby tees should be given a
medal. I feel the same way about the person who designed the matching
cookie cutter. They're adaptable to any color scheme. Cut off the bottom
of the cookie, and you've got yourself a T-shirt for other creative designs.

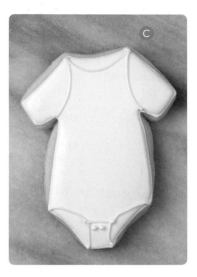

you will need

Monogram Embellishment

Royal Icing (page 28) tinted:
SKY BLUE

Waxed paper

Disposable icing bag

Coupler

Icing tip: #2 or #1

Squeeze bottle

Cookies

Vanilla-Almond Sugar Cookies
(page 22), baby romper shape

Royal Icing (page 28), divided
and tinted (for all three designs):
WHITE • BLACK • FOREST GREEN •
EGG YELLOW

Disposable icing bags (4)

Couplers

Icing tips: #2, #1

Squeeze bottles (4)

Toothpicks

Black food-coloring pen

For the Button Rompers

1 At least a day (and up to 2 weeks) before making the cookies, make the button embellishments. Using the method described on page 18, pipe sky blue icing into circles on waxed paper. Thin the icing and fill in the circles. Let them dry overnight, carefully remove them from the waxed paper, and store in an airtight container until ready to use.

2 Scoop some white icing into a bag and use a #2 tip to outline the rompers Ⓐ. Reserve some white icing in the bag for piping details.

3 Thin the remaining white icing for flooding (as described on page 16). Cover the icing with a damp dish towel and let it sit for several minutes. Gently stir with a silicone spatula and transfer the icing to a squeeze bottle.

4 Fill in the romper outlines with thinned white icing. Use a toothpick to guide icing to the edges and pop air bubbles. Ⓑ

5 Use a #1 tip with white icing to add the romper details. Ⓒ

6 Let the cookies dry uncovered for 6 to 8 hours or overnight, then complete the final details:
→ Use a black food coloring pen to write "cute as a" on the rompers.
→ Use a #1 tip with white icing to add four dots onto the buttons. Attach the buttons to the cookies with a bit of white royal icing. Ⓓ

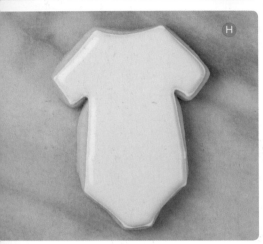

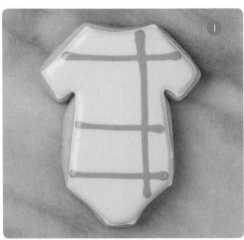

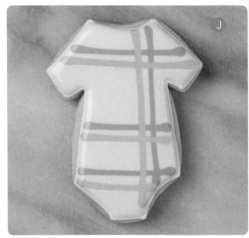

For the Tie Rompers

1 Start the same way as for the previous design, steps 2 through 5. This time, let the cookies dry for at least one hour.

2 Use a #2 tip with black icing to pipe the outline of a tie on the rompers. **E**

3 Thin the blue icing for flooding and prepare as usual. Fill in the ties. **F**

4 Use a #1 tip with green icing to pipe stripes on the tie. Let the cookies dry uncovered for 6 to 8 hours or overnight. **G**

For the Plaid Rompers

1 Use a #2 tip with white icing to outline the rompers.

2 Thin the yellow, blue, and green icings for flooding (as described on page 16). Cover the icings with a damp dish towel and let them sit for several minutes. Gently stir with a silicone spatula and transfer to a squeeze bottle.

3 Working six cookies at a time, fill the rompers with yellow icing. **H** Use a toothpick to guide icing to the edges and pop air bubbles. On top of the wet icing, drop lines in blue and green thinned icing, making a plaid pattern. **I** **J**

4 Use a #1 tip with white icing to pipe on the romper details.

5 Let the cookies dry uncovered for 6 to 8 hours or overnight.

Yellow flowers always remind me of my mom. And as a mom, I can assure you that a bouquet of edible flowers is every bit as welcome as a real one—maybe more so. For a flower assortment, combine this design with the Daisies on page 30.

you will need

Vanilla-Almond Sugar Cookies (page 22), daffodil shape

Royal Icing (page 28), divided and tinted:
EGG YELLOW, LIGHT AND DARK

Disposable icing bag

Coupler

Icing tip: #2

Squeeze bottles (2)

Toothpicks

DAFFODILS

1 Scoop some dark yellow icing into a bag and attach a #2 tip.
→ Outline the daffodil sections: the ruffled top, the center, and around the edges. (A)
→ Reserve some icing in the bag for piping details.

2 Thin the remaining yellow icings for flooding (as described on page 16). Cover them with a damp dishtowel and let them sit for several minutes. Gently stir with a silicone spatula and transfer icing to squeeze bottles as needed.

3 Fill in the outlined areas with thinned icing as follows, using a toothpick to guide it to the edges and pop air bubbles:
→ Use the lighter yellow icing to fill in the ruffled top and the main part of the flower. (B)
→ Use the darker yellow icing to fill in the center of the flower.

4 Let the cookies dry for at least 30 minutes.

5 Use a #2 tip with darker yellow icing to pipe details onto the flower petals.

6 Let the cookies dry uncovered for 6 to 8 hours or overnight.

I "HEART" MOM TATTOOS

Mom might not be a fan of the real thing, but I'm pretty sure that she'll love these tattoo cookies. Outline cookies in black for a graphic look and to make the flood colors really pop!

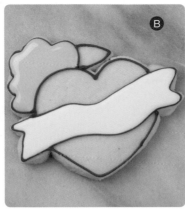

you will need

Vanilla-Almond Sugar Cookies (page 22), tattoo shape (template on page 156)

Royal Icing (page 28), divided and tinted:
BLACK • SKY BLUE • EGG YELLOW • RED • LEAF GREEN

Disposable icing bags (3)

Couplers

Icing tips: #2, #1

Squeeze bottles (3)

Toothpicks

1 Scoop black icing into a bag and attach a #2 tip. Outline the tattoo sections: heart, banner, flower, and leaf. Reserve this bag for piping details. Ⓐ

2 Set aside some of the sky blue icing, then thin the yellow, red, and remaining blue icings for flooding (as described on page 16). Cover the icings with a damp dishtowel and let them sit for several minutes. Gently stir with a silicone spatula and transfer icing to squeeze bottles as needed.

3 Fill in outlined areas with thinned icing as follows, using a toothpick to guide it to the edges and pop air bubbles:
→ Use yellow icing to fill in the banner.
→ Use blue icing to fill in the flower. Ⓑ
→ Use red icing to fill in the heart. Ⓒ

4 Let the cookies dry for at least 1 hour.

5 Pipe on the following details:
→ Use a #2 tip with green icing to fill in the leaf.
→ Use a #1 tip with black icing to pipe "MOM" on the banner. Ⓓ
→ Use a #2 tip with sky blue icing to add curved lines to the flower.

6 Let the cookies dry uncovered for 6 to 8 hours or overnight.

MAMA & BABY BIRDS

PAGE
84

I find that if I try to get too literal with cookie designs, they never look quite right. Therefore, I bring you the combination bluebird/robin redbreast, complete with polka dots and eyelashes.

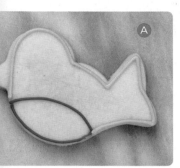   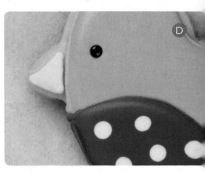

you will need

Vanilla-Almond Sugar Cookies (page 22), bird shapes

Royal Icing (page 28), divided and tinted:
RED • SKY BLUE • WHITE • EGG YELLOW • BLACK

Disposable icing bags (4)

Couplers

Icing tips: #2, #1

Squeeze bottles (3)

Toothpicks

Black food-coloring pen

1 Scoop some red and blue icings into bags and attach #2 tips.
→ Outline the bottom of the birds in red. Return the unused icing to the bowl.
→ Outline the remainder of the body in blue. Save the blue icing in the bag for piping details. Ⓐ

2 Thin the remaining red, blue, and white icings for flooding (as described on page 16). Cover the icings with a damp dishtowel and let them sit for several minutes. Gently stir with a silicone spatula and transfer icing to squeeze bottles as needed.

3 Working six cookies at a time, fill in the outlined areas with thinned icing as follows, using a toothpick to guide it to the edges and pop air bubbles:
→ Use red icing to fill in the mama bird tummies.
→ On top of the wet red icing, drop dots of thinned white icing. (The flat dot technique is described on page 17.) Ⓑ
→ Use red icing to fill in the baby bird tummies.
→ Use blue icing to fill in the bird bodies. Ⓒ

4 Pipe on the following details:
→ Use a #1 tip with yellow icing to pipe the beak.
→ Use a #1 tip with black icing to add an eye. Ⓓ
→ Use a #2 tip with blue icing to pipe the tail and wing details.

5 Let the cookies dry uncovered for 6 to 8 hours or overnight.

6 Use a food-coloring pen to add eyelashes to the mama birds.

QUEEN-FOR-THE-DAY CROWNS

Feel free to treat Mom like a queen every day of the year, but at least roll out the red carpet for her on Mother's Day.

you will need

Chocolate-Hazelnut Cookies (page 24), crown shape

Royal Icing (page 28), divided and tinted:
GOLD • DEEP PINK • ELECTRIC PINK • PURPLE • GREEN

Disposable icing bags (4)

Couplers

Icing tips: #2, #5

Squeeze bottles (3)

Toothpicks

Gold luster dust

Vodka

Small paintbrush

1 Scoop some gold icing into a bag and use a #2 tip to outline the crown in gold. A

2 Return the gold icing to the bowl and thin it for flooding (as described on page 16). Cover the icing with a damp dishtowel and let it sit for several minutes. Gently stir with a silicone spatula and transfer the icing to a squeeze bottle.

3 Fill in the crown with the thinned gold icing. Use a toothpick to guide icing to the edges and pop air bubbles. Let the cookies dry for at least 1 hour.

4 Scoop some deep pink icing into a bag and use a #2 tip to outline a circle on the crown. B

5 Return the deep pink icing to the bowl and thin both pinks for flooding as before. Working six cookies at a time:
→ Use thinned deep pink icing to fill in the circles.
→ On top of the wet icing, pipe a swirl of thinned electric pink icing. C

6 Pipe on the following details:
→ Use a #5 tip with purple icing to pipe the horizontal band.
→ Use a #2 tip with green icing to add a leaf to the flower. D

7 Let the cookies dry uncovered for 6 to 8 hours or overnight.

8 Mix together ¼ teaspoon gold luster dust with several drops of vodka. Brush the mixture onto the crowns using a small, clean paintbrush. (Details on applying luster dust are on page 20.)

EDIBLE COUPONS

This is a really fun gift for the kids to give Dad.
Prepare the cookies the night before, and
then let the kiddos fill in the coupons using a
food-coloring pen.

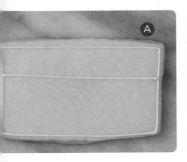

you will need

Vanilla-Almond Sugar Cookies (page 22), coupon shape (template on page 156)

Royal Icing (page 28), divided and tinted:
WHITE • MINT GREEN • BLACK • RED

Disposable icing bags (3)

Couplers

Icing tips: #2, #1

Squeeze bottles (2)

Toothpicks

Black food-coloring pen

1 Scoop some white icing into a bag and attach a #2 tip. Outline the coupon in white and pipe a line across the top part of the cookie. Return unused white icing to the bowl. Ⓐ

2 Thin the white and mint green icings for flooding (as described on page 16). Cover them with a damp dishtowel and let them sit for several minutes. Gently stir with a silicone spatula and transfer icing to squeeze bottles as needed.

3 Fill in the outlined areas with thinned icing as follows, using a toothpick to guide it to the edges and pop air bubbles:
→ Use white icing to fill in the top part of the coupon.
→ Use mint green icing to fill in the bottom part of the coupon. Ⓑ

4 Let the cookies dry for at least 1 hour.

5 Use a #1 tip with black icing to pipe "COUPON" across the top of the cookie. To help with centering, start in the center of the word and work out to the ends. Pipe "For:" on the mint green section.

6 Use a #1 tip with red icing to pipe a heart on the mint green section, and pipe hearts in the O's in the word "COUPON." Let the cookies dry uncovered for 6 to 8 hours or overnight. Ⓒ

7 Let the kids use a black food-coloring pen to fill in the coupon for Dad. Ⓓ

TASTY BIRTHDAYS

Not only will Dad appreciate these custom cookies, but kids will love to see their names and birthdates in icing. Use different shades of pink or blue, or a combination. Because all dads seem to love pie, I use Key Lime Pie Cookies here. Feel free to substitute your dad's favorite.

you will need

Key Lime Pie Cookies (page 25), circles

Key Lime Royal Icing (page 28), divided and tinted:
CHOCOLATE BROWN •
SKY BLUE (IN VARYING SHADES) •
DEEP PINK (IN VARYING SHADES)

Disposable icing bag

Coupler, Icing tips: #2, #1

Squeeze bottles

Toothpicks

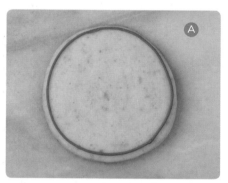

1 Scoop the chocolate brown icing into a bag and use a #2 tip to outline the circles. Reserve the brown icing in the bag for piping details. Ⓐ

2 Thin all of the blue and pink icings for flooding (as described on page 16). Cover the icings with a damp dishtowel and let them sit for several minutes. Gently stir with a silicone spatula and transfer icing to squeeze bottles as needed.

3 Fill in the circles, using the darker shades for the oldest child, down to the lightest for the youngest. Use a toothpick to guide icing to the edges and pop air bubbles. Let the cookies dry for at least 1 hour. Ⓑ

4 Use a #1 tip with the brown icing to pipe the children's names in cursive, starting from one edge and continuing out to the other. Pipe the birthdates below the names.

5 Let the cookies dry uncovered for 6 to 8 hours or overnight.

BEER & HOT DOGS

Beer and hot dog cookies ... they're the
perfect marriage of manly plus cute.
(Tip: For a St. Patrick's Day cookie,
make the beer icing green.)

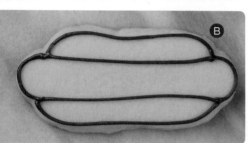

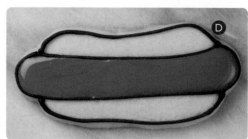

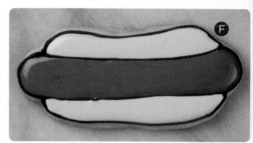

you will need

Vanilla-Almond Sugar Cookies (page 22), beer shape and hot dog shape

Royal Icing (page 28), divided and tinted:
BLACK • WHITE • GOLD MIXED WITH EGG YELLOW • MAROON • IVORY • EGG YELLOW • RED

Disposable icing bags (4)

Couplers

Icing tips: #3, #2

Squeeze bottles (4)

Toothpicks

Optional
Meringue powder

Small paintbrush

Green jimmies

1 Scoop black icing into a bag and attach a #3 tip. Outline sections for the beer mug and foam Ⓐ, and the hot dog and bun. Ⓑ Save this bag for later piping details. Also set aside some white in a bag with a #2 tip.

2 Thin the remaining white and the gold, maroon, and ivory icings for flooding (as described on page 16). Cover the icings with a damp dishtowel and let them sit for several minutes. Gently stir with a silicone spatula and transfer icing to squeeze bottles as needed.

3 Fill in the outlined areas with thinned icing as follows, using a toothpick to guide it to the edges and pop air bubbles:
→ Use gold icing to fill in the beer mug. Ⓒ
→ Use maroon icing to fill in the hot dog. Ⓓ
→ Use white icing to fill in the beer foam and handle. Ⓔ
→ Use ivory icing to fill in the bun. Ⓕ

4 Pipe on the following details:
→ Use a #2 tip with white icing to pipe swirls on the beer foam. Ⓖ
→ Use a #3 tip with black icing to pipe detail lines on the beer mug. Ⓗ

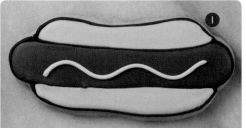

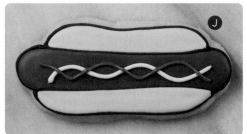

→ Use a #2 tip with yellow or red icing (or both) to add a squiggle of mustard or ketchup onto the hot dogs. **I** **J**

5 Let the cookies dry uncovered for 6 to 8 hours or overnight.

6 If desired, add a bit of relish: Mix together ¼ teaspoon meringue powder with ¼ teaspoon water. Use a small paintbrush to dot on bits of the mixture around the ketchup and mustard. Sprinkle on the green jimmies and shake off the excess. **K** (Details for working with add-ons are on page 19.)

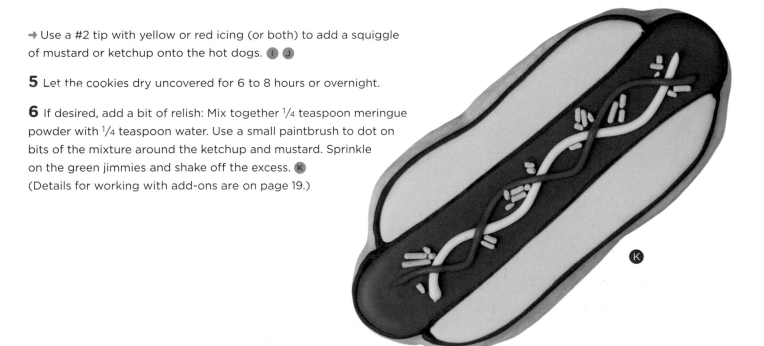

POPSICLES

This is my kind of Popsicle: no drips, no sticky fingers, no last bite falling off the stick and onto the ground. A blogging friend and artist, Renee, taught me the wood grain technique for the sticks.

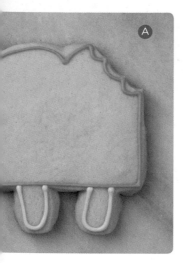
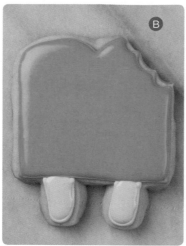
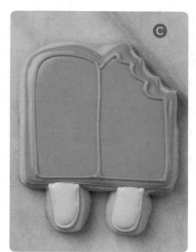

you will need

Vanilla-Almond Sugar Cookies
(page 22), Popsicle shape

Royal Icing (page 28), divided
and tinted:
ORANGE • REGAL PURPLE • IVORY

Disposable icing bags (3)

Couplers

Icing tips: #2

Squeeze bottles (3)

Toothpicks

Small fan paintbrush

Brown gel paste food coloring

Note: For a fun variation, and before baking, use a scalloped-edge
cookie cutter to make a bite mark at the top of some of the cookies.

1 Scoop some of each color icing into bags and attach #2 tips.
→ Outline the tops of the Popsicles, some in orange and some in purple.
Reserve some of both colors in the bags for later piping details.
→ Outline the sticks in ivory. Ⓐ
→ Return leftover icings to their bowls.

2 Thin the remaining orange, purple, and ivory icings for flooding (as
described on page 16). Cover the icings with a damp dishtowel and let
them sit for several minutes. Gently stir with a silicone spatula and
transfer icing to squeeze bottles as needed.

3 Fill in outlined areas with thinned icing as follows, using a toothpick
to guide it to the edges and pop air bubbles:
→ Use orange or purple icings to fill the tops (match the outlines).
→ Use ivory icing to fill in the sticks. Ⓑ

4 Use the reserved orange and purple icing to go over the outlines of
the Popsicles. Ⓒ

5 Let the cookies dry uncovered for 6 to 8 hours or overnight.

6 Trim a fan brush with scissors so that the ends are uneven (some
bristles left long, others trimmed short). On a small plate or tray, mix
together 2 drops of brown gel paste food coloring with 2 drops of water.
Saturate the bristles of the brush in the mixture, then drag the brush
across the plate to wipe off the excess. Starting at the top of the sticks,
drag the fan brush down. Voilà—wood grain! Ⓓ

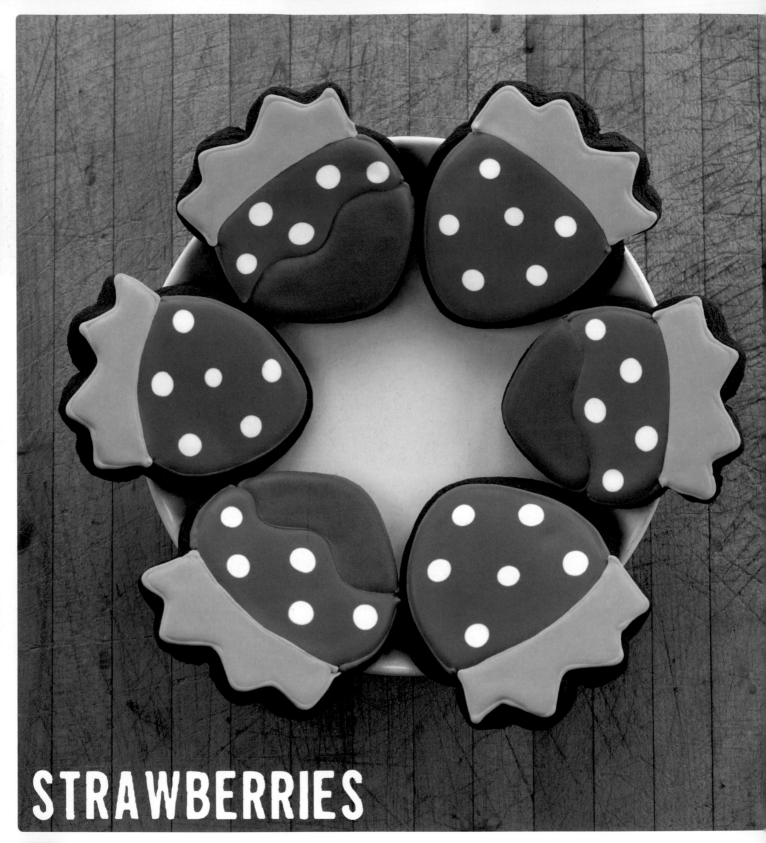

STRAWBERRIES

Strawberries are my favorite fruit. And dipped in chocolate? Be still, my heart.

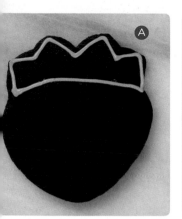  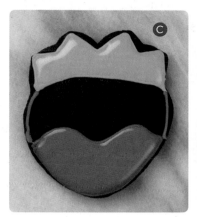 

you will need

Chocolate-Hazelnut Cookies (page 24), strawberry shape

Royal Icing (page 28), divided and tinted:
LEAF GREEN • CHOCOLATE BROWN • RED • WHITE

Disposable icing bags (3)

Couplers

Icing tips: #2

Squeeze bottles (4)

Toothpicks

1 Scoop some of the green, brown, and red icings into bags and attach #2 tips.
→ Outline the tops of the strawberries in green icing. Ⓐ
→ Outline the chocolate-dipped section in brown icing.
→ Outline the remainder of the cookie in red icing. Ⓑ

2 Return all unused icing to the bowls and thin all four colors for flooding (as described on page 16). Cover the icings with a damp dishtowel and let them sit for several minutes. Gently stir with a silicone spatula and transfer icing to squeeze bottles as needed.

3 Fill in the outlined areas with thinned icing as follows, using a toothpick to guide it to the edges and pop air bubbles:
→ Use green icing to fill in the leaves.
→ Use brown icing to fill in the bottoms of the strawberries. Ⓒ

4 Working six cookies at a time:
→ Fill in the tops of the strawberries in red.
→ On top of the wet icing, drop dots of thinned white icing. (The flat dot technique is described on page 17.) Ⓓ

5 Let the cookies dry uncovered for 6 to 8 hours or overnight.

FOURTH OF JULY
FIRECRACKERS

There is something pretty magical about sitting with your family watching fireworks burst across the dark night sky. There's something magical about these cookies, too. They lend themselves to just about every decorating technique you can think of: dots, marbling, sanding sugar, disco dust. The possibilities are endless.

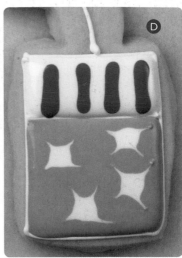

you will need

Vanilla-Almond Sugar Cookies (page 22), firecracker shape

Royal Icing (page 28), divided and tinted:
WHITE • RED • NAVY BLUE

Disposable icing bag

Coupler

Icing tip: #2

Squeeze bottles (3)

Toothpicks

Meringue powder

Small paintbrush

White sanding sugar

1 Scoop some white icing into a bag and attach a #2 tip. Outline the base of the firecracker and divide it into sections as desired. Pipe lines for the wick and spark on the top. Ⓐ

2 Thin the remaining white, red, and blue icings for flooding (as described on page 16). Cover the icings with a damp dishtowel and let them sit for several minutes. Gently stir with a silicone spatula and transfer the icing to squeeze bottles as needed.

3 Working six cookies at a time, fill each section of the firecracker base in your color of choice. Use a toothpick to guide icing to the edges and pop air bubbles.

4 Add the following details, as you like, on top of the wet icing:
→ Dots: Drop dots of thinned icing. (The flat dot technique is described on page 17.) Ⓑ
→ Lines: Add lines of thinned icing.
→ Starbursts: Drop a dot in the center and add circles around it with thinned icing. Drag a toothpick from the center, moving out and back all the away around the circle. (The marbling technique is described on page 18.) Ⓒ
→ Mini starbursts: Drop a large dot with thinned icing. Drag a toothpick out from the center of the dot several times. Ⓓ

5 Let the cookies dry uncovered for 6 to 8 hours or overnight.

6 Mix together ¼ teaspoon meringue powder with ¼ teaspoon water. Brush the wicks with the mixture and sprinkle on the white sanding sugar (as described on page 19). Shake off the excess.

Variation
Instead of the sanding sugar, use rainbow disco dust.

PIRATE BOYS, PARROTS & TREASURE MAPS

A pirate's favorite cookie may be Ships Ahoy (get it?), but these cookies ARRRR sure to win him over. (Speaking like a pirate while making these cookies is totally optional, but very entertaining.)

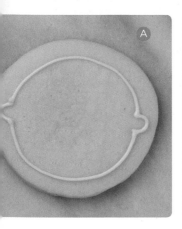
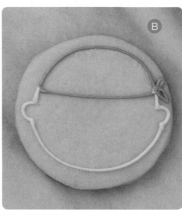

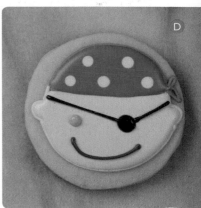

you will need

Vanilla-Almond Sugar Cookies (page 22), circles

Royal Icing (page 28), divided and tinted:
LIGHT COPPER OR WARM BROWN (SKIN TONE) • ROYAL BLUE • WHITE • GREEN OR CHOCOLATE BROWN • BLACK • RED • YELLOW

Disposable icing bags (6)

Couplers

Icing tips: #2, #1

Squeeze bottles (3)

Toothpicks

Pirate Boys

1 Scoop some flesh tone and blue icings into bags and attach #2 tips.
→ Outline the head shape in skin tone icing. Ⓐ
→ Outline the scarf across the top of the head. With a toothpick, scrape off the skin tone outline at the top of the head and go over it with blue. Pipe a tie with blue icing to one side of the scarf. Ⓑ

2 Thin the skin tone, blue, and white icings for flooding (as described on page 16). Cover the icings with a damp dishtowel and let them sit for several minutes. Gently stir with a silicone spatula and transfer icing to squeeze bottles as needed.

3 Fill in the faces with thinned skin tone icing, using a toothpick to guide icing to the edges and pop air bubbles.

4 Working six cookies at a time:
→ Fill in the scarves with thinned blue icing, using a toothpick as before.
→ On top of the wet icing, drop dots of thinned white icing. (The flat dot technique is described on page 17.) Ⓒ

5 Let the cookies dry for at least 1 hour.

6 Pipe on the following details:
→ Use a #2 tip with green or chocolate brown icing to add an eye.
→ Use a #2 tip with black icing to add an eye patch and strap.
→ Use a #2 tip with red icing to pipe a smile. Ⓓ
→ Use a #1 tip with yellow or brown icing to add hair below the edge of the scarf.

7 Let the cookies dry uncovered for 6 to 8 hours or overnight.

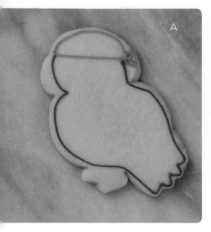
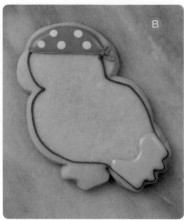
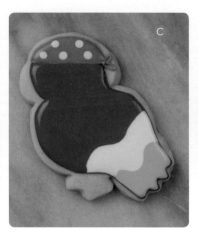

you will need

> Vanilla-Almond Sugar Cookies
> (page 22), parrot shape
>
> Royal Icing (page 28), divided
> and tinted:
> ROYAL BLUE • RED •
> WHITE • EGG YELLOW •
> LEAF GREEN • BLACK
>
> Disposable icing bags (4)
>
> Couplers
>
> Icing tips: #2, #1
>
> Squeeze bottles (5)
>
> Toothpicks

Pirate Parrots

1 Scoop some of the blue and red icings into bags and attach #2 tips.
→ Outline the scarf in blue. Add a tie out to one side.
→ Outline the body of the parrot in red, leaving off the beak. Ⓐ

2 Return the red and blue icings to the bowl, and reserve some yellow icing for piping details. Thin the remaining colors, except black, for flooding (as described on page 16). Cover the icings with a damp dishtowel and let them sit for several minutes. Gently stir with a silicone spatula and transfer icing to squeeze bottles as needed.

3 Working six cookies at a time, add thinned icing as follows, using a toothpick to guide icing to the edges and pop air bubbles:
→ Use blue icing to fill in the scarves.
→ On top of the wet icing, drop dots of white. (The flat dot technique is described on page 17.)
→ Use green icing to fill in the bottom of the tail. Ⓑ
→ Use yellow icing to fill in the middle of the tail.
→ Use red icing to fill in the remainder of the parrot. Ⓒ

4 Pipe on the following details
→ Use a #1 tip with yellow icing to add a beak and feet. Ⓓ
→ Use a #2 tip with black icing to add an eye patch and strap. Ⓔ

5 Let the cookies dry uncovered for 6 to 8 hours or overnight.

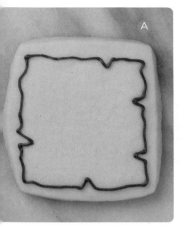
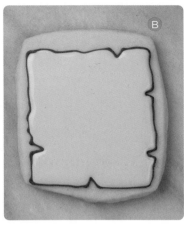

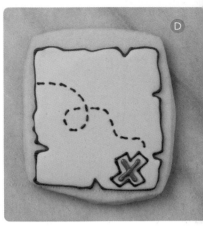

you will need

Vanilla-Almond Sugar Cookies
(page 22), rectangles

Royal Icing (page 28), divided
and tinted:
BLACK • IVORY • RED

Disposable icing bags (2)

Couplers

Icing tips: #2, #1

Squeeze bottle

Toothpicks

Treasure Maps

1 Scoop some black icing into a bag and use a #2 tip to outline the uneven edges of the map. Save icing in the bag for piping details. Ⓐ

2 Thin the ivory icing for flooding (as described on page 16). Cover it with a damp dishtowel and let it sit for several minutes. Gently stir with a silicone spatula and transfer the icing to a squeeze bottle.

3 Fill in the maps with thinned ivory icing. Use a toothpick to guide icing to the edges and pop air bubbles. Let the cookies dry for at least 1 hour. Ⓑ

4 Pipe on the following details:
→ Use a #2 tip with red icing to pipe an X on the map. Ⓒ
→ Use a #1 tip with black icing to pipe dashes, starting at one edge of the cookies and leading to the X. Outline the X. Ⓓ

5 Let the cookies dry uncovered for 6 to 8 hours or overnight.

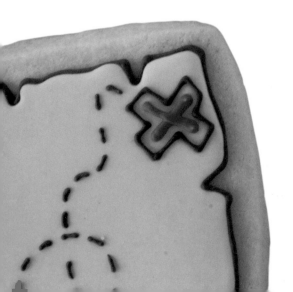

GOING ON A PICNIC

My favorite picnics were always the rainy-day indoor picnics that my kiddo and I would have on the living room floor. Nowadays, I love having an evening picnic at an outdoor concert, when the sun is setting and the heat of the day is over. Whenever you have your picnic, I hope the only ants involved are the ones you piped onto the cookies.

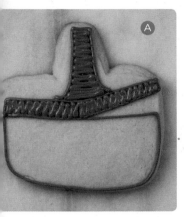
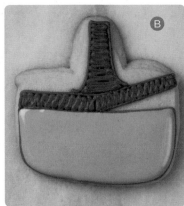

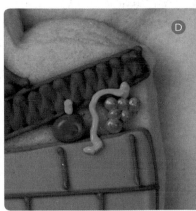

you will need

Vanilla-Almond Sugar Cookies
(page 22), basket shape

Royal Icing (page 28), divided
and tinted:
CHOCOLATE BROWN, LIGHT AND
DARK • RED • REGAL PURPLE •
LEAF GREEN

Disposable icing bags (4)

Couplers

Icing tips: #2, #1, #3

Squeeze bottle

Toothpicks

Picnic Baskets

1 Scoop the dark chocolate brown icing into a bag and attach a #2 tip. Outline the basket, piping half of the lid at an angle. Use a back-and-forth motion to fill in the lid and handle with icing. Save the icing in the bag for piping details. Ⓐ

2 Thin the lighter brown icing for flooding (as described on page 16). Cover the icing with a damp dishtowel and let it sit for several minutes. Gently stir with a silicone spatula and transfer the icing to a squeeze bottle.

3 Fill in the basket bottom with the thinned icing. Use a toothpick to guide icing to the edges and pop air bubbles. Let the cookies dry for at least 1 hour. Ⓑ

4 Pipe on the following details:
→ Use a #1 tip with dark brown icing to pipe the basket detail. Ⓒ
→ Use a #3 tip with red icing to pipe an apple peeking out of the basket.
→ Use a #1 tip with purple icing to pipe grapes next to the apple.
→ Use a #1 tip with green icing to pipe stems on the apple and grapes. Ⓓ

5 Let the cookies dry uncovered for 6 to 8 hours or overnight.

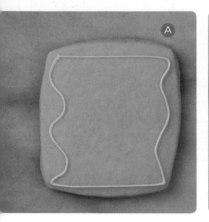 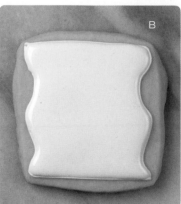 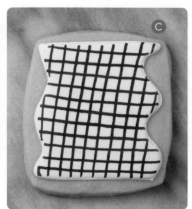 

you will need

Vanilla-Almond Sugar Cookies
(page 22), rectangles

Royal Icing (page 28), divided
and tinted:
WHITE • BLACK

Disposable icing bags (2)

Couplers

Icing tips: #2, #1

Squeeze bottle

Toothpicks

Red food-coloring pen

Picnic Blankets

1 Scoop some white icing into a bag and use a #2 tip to outline the blanket. (A)

2 Thin the remaining white icing for flooding (as described on page 16). Cover the icing with a damp dishtowel and let it sit for several minutes. Gently stir with a silicone spatula and transfer the icing to a squeeze bottle.

3 Fill in the blankets with the thinned white icing. Use a toothpick to guide icing to the edges and pop air bubbles. (B)

4 Let the cookies dry uncovered for 6 to 8 hours or overnight.

5 Use a red food-coloring pen to draw lines for the checked blanket. (C)

TIP *If you store your food-coloring pens in the refrigerator like I do, let them sit out at room temperature for at least 10 minutes to get the most vibrant color.*

6 Use a #1 tip with black icing to add ants marching across the blanket. (D)

LEMONS & LEMONADE

Serve these cookies with a tall, cold glass of lemonade and you have the perfect summertime treat.

PAGE
107

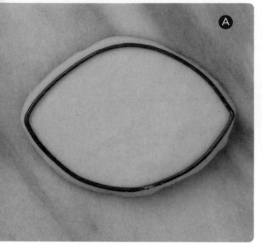
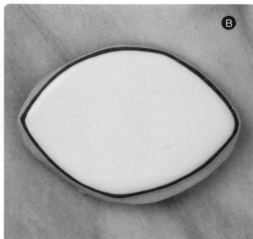
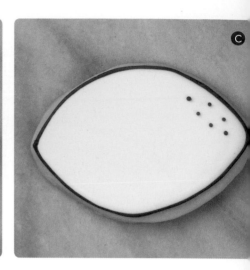

you will need

Lemon Variation Sugar Cookies (page 23), lemon shape

Royal Icing (page 28), divided and tinted:
BLACK • LEMON YELLOW

Disposable icing bag

Coupler

Icing tips: #3, #1

Squeeze bottle

Toothpicks

Lemons

1 Scoop the black icing into a bag and use a #3 tip to outline the lemon. Save the remaining black icing in the bag for piping details. Ⓐ

2 Let the cookies dry for at least 1 hour.

3 Thin the yellow icing for flooding (as described on page 16). Cover the icing with a damp dishtowel and let it sit for several minutes. Gently stir with a silicone spatula and transfer the icing to a squeeze bottle.

4 Fill in the lemons with thinned yellow icing. Use a toothpick to guide icing to the edges and pop air bubbles. Ⓑ

5 Switch the black icing to a #1 tip and add dot detail to one corner. Ⓒ

6 Let the cookies dry uncovered for 6 to 8 hours or overnight.

LEMONS & LEMONADE

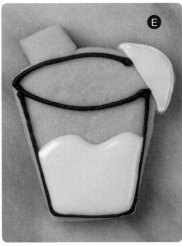

you will need

Lemon Variation Sugar Cookies (page 23), glass shape (template on page 156)

Royal Icing (page 28), divided and tinted:
LEMON YELLOW, LIGHT AND DARK • BLACK • WHITE • RED

Disposable icing bags (4)

Couplers

Icing tips: #2, #3, #46 basket weave or #6, #1

Squeeze bottles (2)

Toothpicks

Glasses of Lemonade

1 Scoop some dark lemon yellow and black icing into bags.
→ Use a #2 tip with yellow icing to outline the lemon wedge.
→ Use a #3 tip with black icing to outline the glass. **D**

2 Let the cookies dry for at least 1 hour.

3 Reserve some of the white icing for piping details. Thin the lighter yellow and remaining white icings for flooding (as described on page 16). Cover the icings with a damp dishtowel and let them sit for several minutes. Gently stir with a silicone spatula and transfer the icing to squeeze bottles as needed.

4 Fill in the outlined areas with thinned icing as follows, using a toothpick to guide it to the edges and pop air bubbles:
→ Use light yellow icing to fill in the lemon wedges. Fill in each lemonade glass almost to the top of the rim, but not quite. **E**
→ Use white icing to fill in the remainder of each glass. **F**

5 Pipe on the following details:
→ Use the plain side of a #46 basket weave tip with white icing to add a straw. Alternately, use a plain tip with a larger opening, such as a #6.
→ Use a #1 tip with red icing to add stripes to the straws. **G**
→ Use a #1 tip with yellow icing to go over the outline and add sections to the lemon wedges.

6 Let the cookies dry uncovered for 6 to 8 hours or overnight.

BACK-TO-SCHOOL CRAYONS & RULER

Use any colors you like here. These cookies are perfect for personalizing with either your child's name or the teacher's name.

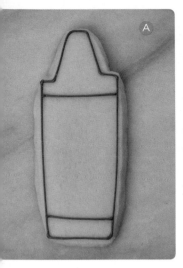

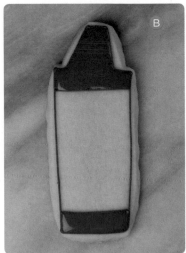

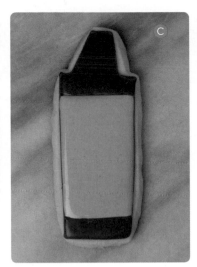

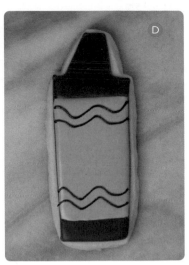

you will need

Vanilla-Almond Sugar Cookies (page 22), crayon shape

Royal Icing (page 28), divided and tinted:
RED, LIGHT AND DARK • **BLUE, LIGHT AND DARK** • **BLACK**

Disposable icing bags (3)

Couplers

Icing tips: #2, #1

Squeeze bottles (4)

Toothpicks

Crayons

1 Scoop some of the dark red and dark blue icings into bags and attach a #2 tip. Outline some crayons in red and some in blue, dividing the tip and bottom into sections. **A**

2 Return the icings to the bowls and thin all red and blue icings for flooding (as described on page 16). Cover the icings with a damp dishtowel and let them sit for several minutes. Gently stir with a silicone spatula and transfer icing to squeeze bottles as needed.

3 Fill in the outlined areas with thinned icing as follows, using a toothpick to guide it to the edges and pop air bubbles:
→ Use the darker icings for the crayon tips and bottoms. **B**
→ Use the lighter icings to fill in the wrapper area. **C**

4 Let the cookies dry for at least 1 hour, then pipe on the following details:
→ Use a #2 tip with black icing to pipe wavy lines on each end of the crayons. **D**
→ Switch to a #1 tip with black icing to pipe the letters in the center of the crayon.

5 Let the cookies dry uncovered for 6 to 8 hours or overnight.

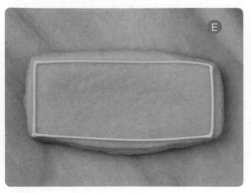 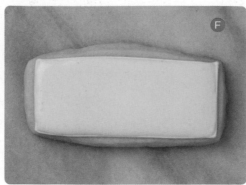 

you will need

Vanilla-Almond Sugar Cookies
(page 22), rectangles

Royal Icing (page 28), divided
and tinted:
EGG YELLOW • BLACK

Disposable icing bags (2)

Couplers

Icing tips: #2, #1

Squeeze bottle

Toothpicks

Rulers

1 Scoop some yellow icing into a bag and use a #2 tip to outline the rulers. E

2 Return the yellow icing to the bowl and thin it for flooding (as described on page 16). Cover the icing with a damp dishtowel and let it sit for several minutes. Gently stir with a silicone spatula and transfer the icing to a squeeze bottle.

3 Fill in the rulers with thinned yellow icing. Use a toothpick to guide icing to the edges and pop air bubbles. Let the cookies dry for at least 1 hour. F

4 Use a #1 tip with black icing to add lines and numbers to the rulers. G

5 Let the cookies dry uncovered for 6 to 8 hours or overnight.

BLACK CATS

No seven years of bad luck here!
These kitties are nothing but sweet.
See the notes on page 14 for how to
mix a rich black icing.

A

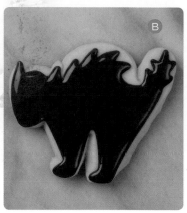

B

C

D

you will need

**Vanilla-Almond Sugar Cookies
(page 22), cat shapes**

**Royal Icing (page 28), divided
and tinted:**
BLACK • ORANGE • GREEN • PINK

Disposable icing bags (4)

Couplers

Icing tips: #2, #1

Squeeze bottles (2)

Toothpicks

1 Scoop some black icing into a bag and use a #2 tip to outline the cats in black. Reserve some black icing in the bag for piping details.

2 Thin the remaining black icing for flooding (as described on page 16). Cover the icing with a damp dishtowel and let it sit for several minutes. Gently stir with a silicone spatula and transfer the icing to a squeeze bottle.

3 Fill in the cats with the thinned black icing. Use a toothpick to guide icing to the edges and pop air bubbles. Let the cookies dry for at least 1 hour. (A) (B)

4 Pipe on the following details:

→ Use a #2 tip with orange icing to add a ribbon on the sitting cats.

→ Use a #1 tip with green icing to add eyes to the cats. Make the eyes round for the sitting cats and oblong for the scary ones. C D

→ Use a #1 tip with black icing to add pupils to the eyes.

→ Use a #1 tip with pink icing to add noses. E F

→ Use a #1 tip with black icing to add whiskers. Add a zigzag detail on the back of the scary cats. G

→ Add small black dots to the orange ribbon. H

5 Let the cookies dry uncovered for 6 to 8 hours or overnight.

ARTFUL TEACHER APPRECIATION

Forgo the coffee mugs and candles for teacher appreciation this year. (I know I've given my share.) Make these cookies with your kids as a showcase for their artwork, and give their teachers something really sweet and personal.

you will need

Vanilla-Almond Sugar Cookies
(page 22), circles

Royal Icing (page 28), divided
and tinted:
WHITE ● EGG YELLOW

Disposable icing bags (2)

Couplers

Icing tips: #2, #15 star

Squeeze bottle

Toothpicks

Food-coloring pens

TIP *Make several extra cookies. Encourage the kids to use a light touch with the pens. While kids get used to using the pen, they may poke a few holes through the icing. Casualties can be eaten, though, and that makes the decorating more fun.*

1 Scoop some white icing into a bag and use a #2 tip to outline the circles in white. Return the unused white icing to the bowl. Ⓐ

2 Thin the white icing for flooding (as described on page 16). Cover the icing with a damp dishtowel and let it sit for several minutes. Gently stir with a silicone spatula and transfer the icing to a squeeze bottle.

3 Fill in the circles with white icing. Use a toothpick to guide icing to the edges and pop air bubbles. Let the cookies dry for 6 to 8 hours or overnight.

4 Once the cookies are dry, have the kids use food-coloring markers to draw pictures and write on the cookies. Ⓑ

5 Use a #15 star tip with yellow icing to pipe a border onto the cookies. Use a pulsing motion to get the ruffled effect. Ⓒ

6 Let the cookies dry uncovered for 6 to 8 hours or overnight.

FOR A "POPULAR" TEACHER

I'm a big believer in sending cookies to school for teachers. I'm not going to say that it will raise your child's grade, but it doesn't hurt. Use the adorable template on page 157, created by Melissa Wilson of www.domesticatedlady.com and Kate Hadfield of www.katehadfielddesigns.com, as a bag topper for gift giving.

you will need

Vanilla-Almond Sugar Cookies
(page 22), candy corn shape

Royal Icing (page 28), divided
and tinted:
RED • WHITE • EGG YELLOW

Disposable icing bags (2)

Couplers

Icing tips: #2, #1

Squeeze bottles (3)

Toothpicks

1 Scoop some red and white icings into bags and attach #2 tips.
→ Outline the popcorn boxes in red icing. Pipe a circle in the middle for the popcorn label. Reserve some red icing in the bag for piping details.
→ Outline several pieces of popcorn in white icing above the box shape. Return unused white icing to the bowl. Ⓐ

2 Thin the remaining red, white, and yellow icings for flooding (as described on page 16). Cover the icings with a damp dishtowel and let them sit for several minutes. Gently stir with a silicone spatula and transfer icing to squeeze bottles as needed.

3 Working six cookies at a time, fill in outlined areas with thinned icing as follows, using a toothpick to guide it to the edges and pop air bubbles:
→ Use white icing to fill in the boxes, excluding the circle in the middle.
→ On top of the wet white icing, add lines of thinned red icing. Ⓑ
→ Use white and yellow icing to fill in the popcorn pieces. Use a toothpick to swirl the colors together slightly.
→ Use yellow icing to fill in the circle. Ⓒ

4 Let the cookies dry for at least 1 hour.

5 Use a #1 tip with red icing to pipe "popcorn" in the center circle. Ⓓ

6 Let the cookies dry uncovered for 6 to 8 hours or overnight.

SWEET SQUIRRELS

I may not like the squirrels that try to hijack my birdfeeder, but these squirrels, I love. Make them with or without the sanding sugar tails. (I vote for with.)

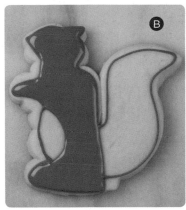

you will need

Vanilla-Almond Sugar Cookies
(page 22), squirrel shape

Royal Icing (page 28), divided
and tinted:
BROWN, LIGHT AND DARK • BLACK

Disposable icing bags (2)

Couplers

Icing tips: #2, #1

Squeeze bottles (2)

Toothpicks

Meringue powder

Small paintbrush

White sanding sugar

1 Scoop some dark brown icing into a bag and attach a #2 tip. Outline the squirrel bodies, sectioning off the tail and a tummy. Reserve some dark brown icing in the bag for piping details. Ⓐ

2 Thin the remaining dark and light brown icings for flooding (as described on page 16). Cover the icings with a damp dishtowel and let them sit for several minutes. Gently stir with a silicone spatula and transfer both icings to squeeze bottles.

3 Fill in the main body of the squirrel with dark brown icing. Use a toothpick to guide icing to the edges and pop air bubbles. Ⓑ

4 Working six cookies at a time:
→ Fill in the tummy and tail with light brown icing, using a toothpick as before.
→ On top of the wet icing, pipe a line of dark brown on the tail. Ⓒ

5 Pipe on the following details:
→ Use a #2 tip with dark brown icing to pipe lines for the arm and leg. Ⓓ
→ Use a #1 tip with black icing to add a nose and eye.

6 Let the cookies dry uncovered for 6 to 8 hours or overnight.

7 Mix together ¼ teaspoon meringue powder with ¼ teaspoon water. Brush the tails and tummies with the mixture and sprinkle on the white sanding sugar (as described on page 19). Shake off the excess.

PUMPKINS

My sister likes to tease me because once
September rolls around, I am pumpkin
obsessed. Pumpkin lattes, pumpkin muffins,
pumpkin patches ... why not pumpkin cookies?

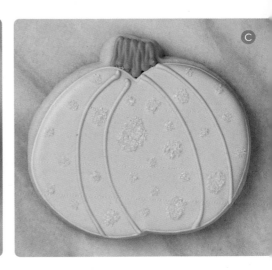

you will need

Vanilla-Almond Sugar Cookies (page 22), pumpkin shape

Royal Icing (page 28), divided and tinted:
IVORY • AVOCADO GREEN • ORANGE • BROWN

Disposable icing bags (4)

Couplers

Icing tips: #2

Squeeze bottles (3)

Toothpicks

Meringue powder

Small paintbrush

White sanding sugar

1 Scoop some of each icing color into bags and attach #2 tips.
→ Outline the pumpkins in ivory, green, and orange. Reserve some of each color for piping details.
→ Outline the stems in brown. Ⓐ

2 Thin the ivory, green, and orange icings for flooding (as described on page 16). Cover the icings with a damp dishtowel and let them sit for several minutes. Gently stir with a silicone spatula and transfer icing to squeeze bottles as needed.

3 Fill in the pumpkins with the matching thinned icing. Use a toothpick to guide icing to the edges and pop air bubbles.

4 Use the reserved icing to pipe lines on the pumpkins. Let the cookies dry uncovered for 6 to 8 hours or overnight. Ⓑ

5 Mix together ¼ teaspoon meringue powder with ¼ teaspoon water. Brush the mixture wherever you would like the sanding sugar to stick. Sprinkle on the white sanding sugar (as described on page 19). Shake off the excess. Ⓒ

SPIDER WEBS

Making spider webs may look like cookie magic, but it's incredibly easy. The only tool you need is a toothpick!

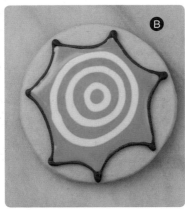

you will need

Vanilla-Almond Sugar Cookies (page 22), circles

Royal Icing (page 28), divided and tinted:
BLACK • ORANGE • WHITE

Disposable icing bag

Coupler

Icing tips: #3, #7, #1

Squeeze bottles (2)

Toothpicks

Meringue powder

Small paintbrush

Black nonpareils

1 Scoop some black icing into a bag and use a #3 tip to outline the outer edge of the spider web. Reserve some black icing in the bag for piping details. Let the cookies dry for at least 1 hour. Ⓐ

2 Thin the orange and white icings for flooding (as described on page 16). Cover the icings with a damp dishtowel and let them sit for several minutes. Gently stir with a silicone spatula and transfer icing to squeeze bottles as needed.

3 To make the inner web, work six cookies at a time as follows:
→ Fill in the webs with either one of the thinned icings. Use a toothpick to guide icing to the edges and pop air bubbles.
→ On top of the wet icing, use the other thinned icing color to add 3 circles. Ⓑ
→ Starting in the middle of the cookie, drag a toothpick out to the web points. Wipe the toothpick off after each drag. (Details on the marbling technique are found on page 18.) Ⓒ

4 Let the cookies dry for at least 1 hour, then pipe on the following details:
→ Switch the black icing bag to a #7 tip. Add a spider body on top of the webs; the large tip will make a black filled-in dot, so no flooding will be needed.
→ Switch to a #1 tip to add legs to the spider. Ⓓ

5 Let the cookies dry for 6 to 8 hours or overnight.

6 Mix together ¼ teaspoon meringue powder with ¼ teaspoon water. Brush the mixture onto the spider bodies. Sprinkle on the nonpareils (as described on page 19). Shake off the excess.

7 Let the cookies dry for about 30 minutes.

DÍA DE LOS MUERTOS

A holiday primarily celebrated in Mexico, the Day of the Dead is a day dedicated to remembering and celebrating dearly departed loved ones. You'll see bright flowers, dancing, and, of course, plenty of food.

you will need

Chocolate-Hazelnut Cookies (page 24), skull shape

Royal Icing (page 28), divided and tinted:
WHITE • RED • PINK • GREEN • BLUE • YELLOW

Disposable icing bags (6)

Couplers

Icing tips: #2, #1

Squeeze bottle

Toothpicks

1 Scoop some white icing into a bag and use a #2 tip to outline the skulls. Return any unused white icing to the bowl. Ⓐ

2 Thin the remaining white icing for flooding (as described on page 16). Cover the icing with a damp dishtowel and let it sit for several minutes. Gently stir with a silicone spatula and transfer the icing to a squeeze bottle.

3 Fill in the skull outlines with the thinned white icing. Use a toothpick to guide icing to the edges and pop air bubbles. Let the cookies dry for at least 30 minutes. Ⓑ

4 Scoop the remaining colors into bags and attach #1 tips. Decorate the skulls as you like. There are no rules here; just use your imagination. Here are the basics:
→ Pipe upside-down hearts for the noses. Ⓒ
→ Outline flowers for the eyes, then fill with a contrasting color.
→ Add teeth with simple lines.
→ Decorate the rest of the skull with hearts, swirls, flowers, and dots. Ⓓ

5 Let the cookies dry uncovered for 6 to 8 hours or overnight.

AUTUMN LEAVES

We get a lot of pine needles in the fall here in Texas, not the glorious fall colors of the Northeast. I like to pretend with cookies. Take that, Vermont!

you will need

Chocolate-Hazelnut Cookies (page 24), leaf shape

Royal Icing (page 28), divided and tinted:
BURGUNDY (MAROON MIXED WITH RED) • ORANGE • GOLD • BROWN

Disposable icing bag

Coupler

Icing tip: #2

Squeeze bottles (4)

Toothpicks

White sanding sugar

Meringue powder

Small paintbrush

1 Scoop some burgundy icing into a bag and use a #2 tip to outline the leaves. Reserve some burgundy icing in the bag for later piping details.

2 Thin the remaining burgundy, orange, gold, and brown icings for flooding (as described on page 16). Cover the icings with a damp dishtowel and let them sit for several minutes. Gently stir with a silicone spatula and transfer icing to squeeze bottles as needed.

3 Working six to eight cookies at a time, fill in the leaf outlines with the thinned burgundy icing. Use a toothpick to guide icing to the edges and pop air bubbles.

4 On top of the wet icing, drop dots of thinned icing in the other colors. (The flat dot technique is described on page 17.) For any sanding sugar leaves you plan to make, omit the dots.

5 Let the cookies dry uncovered for 6 to 8 hours or overnight.

6 To make burgundy sanding sugar, pour white sanding sugar into a lidded container. Add a drop of red and a drop of maroon food coloring and shake vigorously until the coloring is completely incorporated into the sugar.

7 Mix together 1/4 teaspoon meringue powder with 1/4 teaspoon water. Brush the mixture onto the plain leaves. Sprinkle on the burgundy sanding sugar (as described on page 19). Shake off the excess.

A SLICE OF PUMPKIN PIE

Shake things up a little this year with pumpkin pie cookies for Thanksgiving.

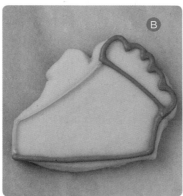

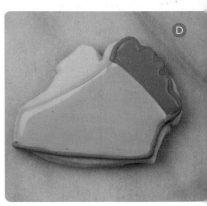

you will need

Vanilla-Almond Sugar Cookies (page 22), pie slice (template on page 156)

Royal Icing (page 28), divided and tinted:
BROWN • ORANGE • WHITE

Disposable icing bags (3)

Couplers

Icing tips: #3, #2

Squeeze bottles (3)

Toothpicks

Meringue powder

Small paintbrush

White sanding sugar

1 Scoop some brown and orange icings into bags.
→ Use a #3 tip with brown icing to outline the top crust of the pie in brown, making a scalloped line for the edge. Ⓐ
→ Use a #2 tip with orange icing to outline the pie wedge. Reserve some of this icing for piping details. Ⓑ

2 Thin the remaining orange and brown icing for flooding (as described on page 16). Cover the icing with a damp dishtowel and let it sit for several minutes. Gently stir with a silicone spatula and transfer icing to squeeze bottles as needed.

3 Fill in the outlined areas with thinned icing as follows, using a toothpick to guide it to the edges and pop air bubbles:
→ Use brown icing to fill in the crust. Ⓒ
→ Use orange icing to fill in the pie wedge. Ⓓ

4 Let the cookies dry for at least 1 hour.

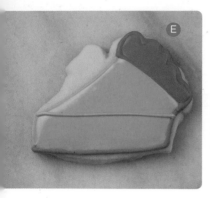
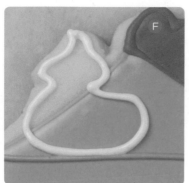

5 Pipe on the following details:

→ Use the reserved orange icing and a #2 tip to pipe a line across the middle of the pie. Ⓔ

→ Use a #2 tip with white icing to outline the whipped cream. Ⓕ

6 Thin and prepare the remaining white icing for flooding as before. Transfer the icing to a squeeze bottle and fill in the whipped cream outline, using a toothpick. Ⓖ

7 Let the cookies dry uncovered for 6 to 8 hours or overnight.

8 Mix together ¼ teaspoon meringue powder with ¼ teaspoon water. Brush the mixture onto the top crust. Sprinkle on the sanding sugar (as described on page 19). Shake off the excess. Ⓗ

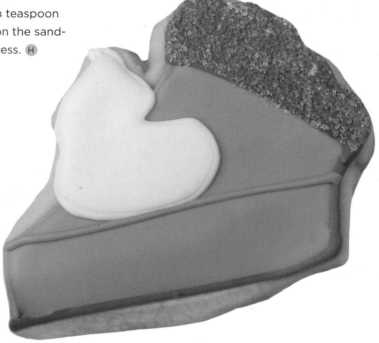

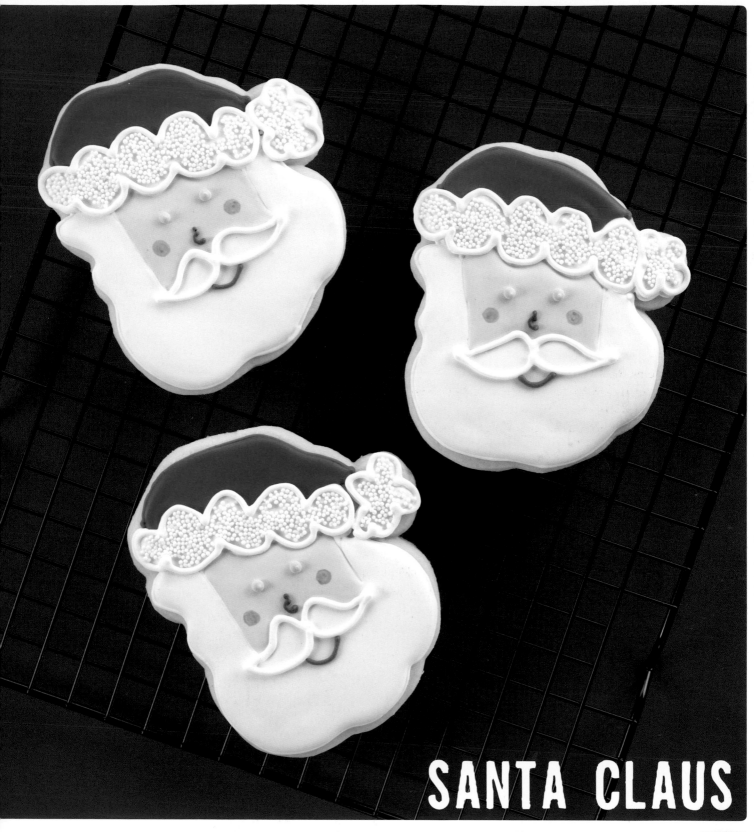

SANTA CLAUS

How can you not love Santa?
He's jolly, he brings presents,
and he loves cookies.
Mrs. Claus married well.

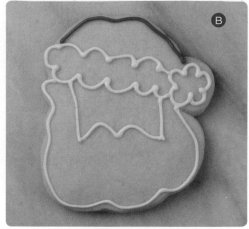

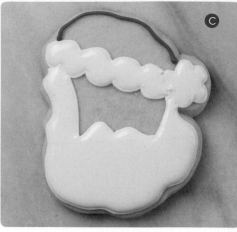

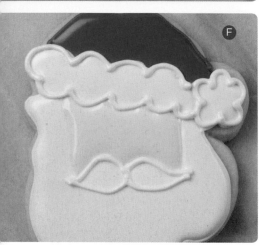

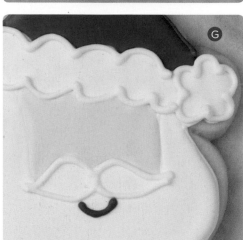

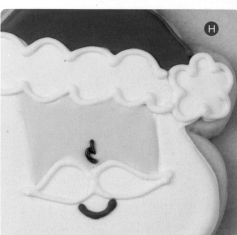

you will need

Vanilla-Almond Sugar Cookies (page 22), Santa face shape

Royal Icing (page 28), divided and tinted:
WHITE • RED • LIGHT COPPER (FOR FLESH TONE) • BLACK • SKY BLUE

Disposable icing bags (4)

Couplers

Icing tips: #2, #1

Squeeze bottles (3)

Toothpicks

Meringue powder

Small paintbrush

White nonpareils

Pink food-coloring pen

1 Scoop some white and red icings into bags and attach #2 tips.
→ Outline Santa's hat trim, beard, and face with white icing. Ⓐ
→ Outline Santa's hat with red icing. Ⓑ
→ Reserve some of both icings for piping details.

2 Thin the remaining white, red, and copper icings for flooding (as described on page 16). Cover the icings with a damp dishtowel and let them sit for several minutes. Gently stir with a silicone spatula and transfer icing to squeeze bottles as needed.

3 Fill in the outlined areas with thinned icing as follows, using a toothpick to guide it to the edges and pop air bubbles:
→ Use white icing to fill in the hat trim and beard. Ⓒ
→ Use red icing to fill in the top of the hat. Ⓓ
→ Use copper icing to fill in the face. Ⓔ

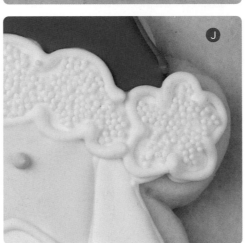

4 Pipe on the following details:

→ Use a #2 tip with white icing to add a moustache and go over the outline of the hat trim. F

→ Use a #1 tip with red icing to add a mouth. G

→ Use a #1 tip with black icing to add a nose. H

→ Use a #2 tip with blue icing to add eyes. I

5 Let the cookies dry uncovered for 6 to 8 hours or overnight.

6 Mix together 1/4 teaspoon meringue powder with 1/4 teaspoon water. Brush the hat trim with the mixture and sprinkle on white nonpareils (as described on page 19). Shake off the excess. J

7 Use a pink food-coloring pen to add rosy cheeks. K

MUGS OF COCOA

Even if it's 70°F in my home state of Texas, I still want to cuddle up with a warm cup of cocoa with marshmallows by a crackling fire—quite possibly while running the air conditioning.

you will need

Chocolate-Hazelnut Cookies
(page 24), mug shape (template
on page 156)

Royal Icing (page 28), divided
and tinted:
SKY BLUE • CHOCOLATE BROWN
• RED

Disposable icing bags (2)

Couplers

Icing tips: #3, #2

Squeeze bottles (2)

Toothpicks

Mini-marshmallows

1 Scoop some sky blue icing into a bag and use a #3 tip to outline the mug. Pipe an oval shape at the top for the cocoa. Ⓐ

2 Thin the remaining blue and brown icings for flooding (as described on page 16). Cover the icings with a damp dishtowel and let them sit for several minutes. Gently stir with a silicone spatula and transfer icing to squeeze bottles as needed.

3 Fill in the outlined areas with thinned icing as follows, using a toothpick to guide it to the edges and pop air bubbles:
➜ Use blue icing to fill in the mug.
➜ Use brown icing to fill in the cocoa. Ⓑ

4 Let the cookies dry for at least 30 minutes.

5 Scoop some red icing into a bag and use a #2 tip to add details to the mug. Ⓒ

6 Let the cookies dry uncovered for 6 to 8 hours or overnight.

7 Use a sharp pair of kitchen scissors to cut the marshmallows in half lengthwise. Dab a bit of royal icing onto the cut side of the marshmallows and press them onto the cocoa. Ⓓ

Variation
Thin white royal icing for flooding. After filling in the thinned, brown icing, add a white swirl. Omit the marshmallows.

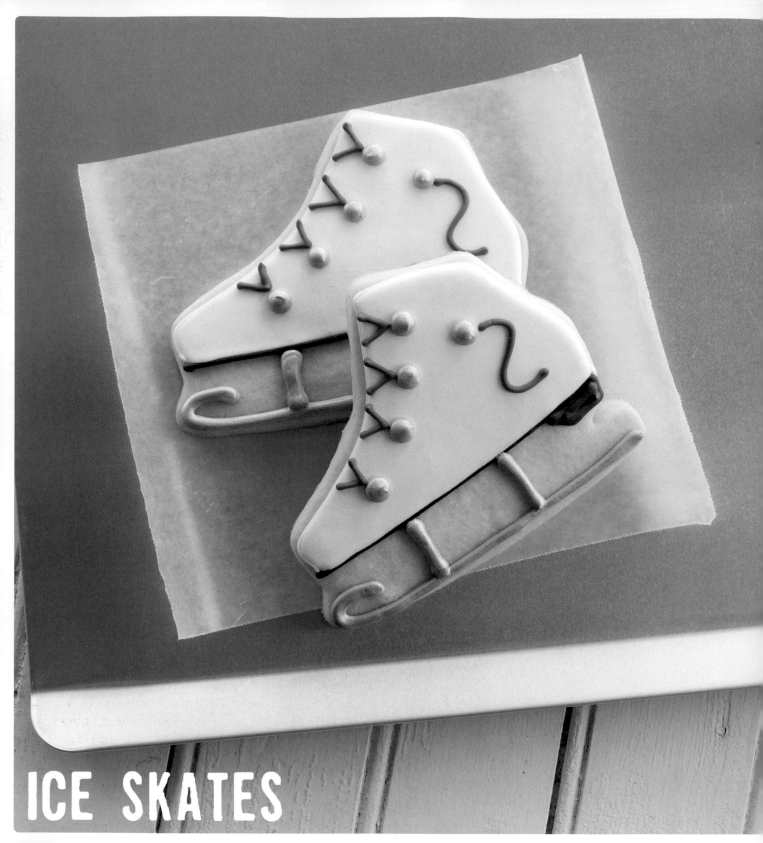

ICE SKATES

I like the idea of ice skating more than I like actually doing it. I'm perfectly content to watch the girls in sparkly outfits twirl on the ice while I munch cookies.

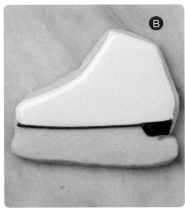

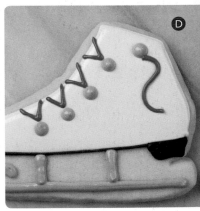

you will need

Vanilla-Almond Sugar Cookies (page 22), ice skate shape

Royal Icing (page 28), divided and tinted:
BLACK • WHITE • GRAY (MADE USING BLACK) • RED

Disposable icing bags (4)

Couplers

Icing tips: #3, #2, #5

Squeeze bottle

Toothpicks

Silver luster dust

Vodka

Small paintbrush

1 Scoop some black and white icings into bags.

→ Use a #3 tip with black icing to outline the sole and heel of the skate.

→ Use a #2 tip with white icing to outline the remainder of the skate. Ⓐ

2 Thin the remaining white icing for flooding (as described on page 16). Cover the icing with a damp dishtowel and let it sit for several minutes. Gently stir with a silicone spatula and transfer the icing to a squeeze bottle.

3 Fill in the skates with the thinned icing. Use a toothpick to guide icing to the edges and pop air bubbles. Let the cookies dry for at least 1 hour. Ⓑ

4 Pipe on the following details:

→ Use a #5 tip with gray icing to add the blade and holes for the laces. Ⓒ

→ Use a #2 tip with red icing to add laces. Ⓓ

5 Let the cookies dry uncovered for 6 to 8 hours or overnight.

6 Add the luster dust to the gray icing: Mix together ¼ teaspoon silver luster dust with several drops of vodka. Brush the mixture onto the blades and the lace holes using a small, clean paintbrush. (Details on applying luster dust are on page 20.)

UNDER THE MISTLETOE

At Christmastime, my mom always hung a sprig of fresh mistletoe in our doorway. I spent my teenage years standing under it hoping for Rick Springfield to ring our doorbell.

you will need

Vanilla-Almond Sugar Cookies (page 22), circles

Royal Icing (page 28), divided and tinted:
GREEN, LIGHT AND DARK • RED • WHITE

Disposable icing bags (4)

Couplers

Icing tips: #2, #1

Squeeze bottles (2)

Toothpicks

1 Scoop some light green icing into a bag and use a #2 tip to outline the circle.

2 Thin the remaining light green icing for flooding (as described on page 16). Cover the icing with a damp dishtowel and let it sit for several minutes. Gently stir with a silicone spatula and transfer the icing to a squeeze bottle.

3 Fill in the circle with the thinned icing. Use a toothpick to guide icing to the edges and pop air bubbles. Let the cookies dry for at least 1 hour. Ⓐ

4 Scoop some red icing into a bag and use a #2 tip to outline the bow in red. Ⓑ

5 Thin the remaining red icing for flooding, and transfer it to a squeeze bottle. Fill in the bows with the thinned red icing, using a toothpick as before. Ⓒ

6 Pipe on the following details:
→ Use a #1 tip with dark green icing to pipe branches and leaves.
→ Use a #1 tip with white icing to add berries. Ⓓ

7 Let the cookies dry uncovered for 6 to 8 hours or overnight.

HOLLY JOLLY COOKIES

Red disco dust is what I imagine Dorothy's shoes were sprinkled with. It's magical.

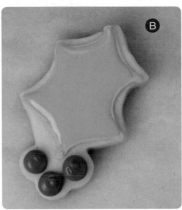

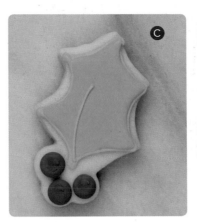

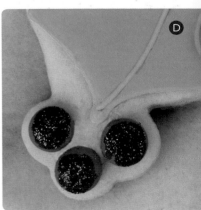

you will need

Vanilla-Almond Sugar Cookies (page 22), holly shape

Royal Icing (page 28), divided and tinted:
LEAF GREEN • RED

Disposable icing bags (2)

Couplers

Icing tips: #2, #5

Squeeze bottle

Toothpicks

Meringue powder

Small paintbrush

Red disco dust

1 Scoop some green icing into a bag and use a #2 tip to outline the holly leaf. Reserve some of this icing for piping details. Ⓐ

2 Thin the remaining green icing for flooding (as described on page 16). Cover the icing with a damp dishtowel and let it sit for several minutes. Gently stir with a silicone spatula and transfer the icing to a squeeze bottle.

3 Fill in the leaves with the thinned green icing. Use a toothpick to guide icing to the edges and pop air bubbles.

4 Pipe on the following details:
→ Use a #5 tip with red icing to add holly berries. Ⓑ
→ Use a #2 tip with green icing to add a line down the center of the leaf. Ⓒ

5 Let the cookies dry uncovered for 6 to 8 hours or overnight.

6 Add disco dust to the berries: Mix together 1/4 teaspoon meringue powder with 1/4 teaspoon water. Brush the berries with the mixture and sprinkle on red disco dust (as described on page 20). Shake off the excess. Use a dry paintbrush to brush away any stray sparkles. Ⓓ

Variation
Substitute red sanding sugar for the disco dust.

SNOWFLAKES

A small tree covered with gingerbread
cookie ornaments makes a darling
and fragrant centerpiece (if you don't
eat them all first)!

you will need

> Gingerbread Cookies (page 26), circles (see note)
>
> Royal Icing (page 28), tinted: WHITE
>
> Disposable icing bag
>
> Couplers
>
> Icing tips: #2, #1
>
> Squeeze bottle
>
> Toothpicks
>
> Meringue powder
>
> Small paintbrush
>
> White sanding sugar
>
> Ribbon

Note: Before baking, use a straw to poke holes in the cookies for the ribbon. Once the cookies are removed from the oven, use a straw to poke the hole again in the same place. (It will have closed up a little during baking.)

1 Scoop some white icing into a bag and use a #2 tip to outline the circles and the cut-out holes. Reserve some of this icing for later piping details.

2 Thin the remaining white icing for flooding (as described on page 16). Cover the icing with a damp dishtowel and let it sit for several minutes. Gently stir with a silicone spatula and transfer the icing to a squeeze bottle.

3 Fill in the circles with the thinned white icing. Use a toothpick to guide icing to the edges and pop air bubbles. **A**

4 Use a #1 tip with the white icing to add the snowflake designs. **B**

5 Let the cookies dry uncovered for 6 to 8 hours or overnight.

6 Mix together 1/4 teaspoon meringue powder with 1/4 teaspoon water. Brush the snowflake design with the mixture and sprinkle on white sanding sugar (as described on page 19). Shake off the excess. **C**

7 Thread a ribbon through the hole and package or hang as desired.

Variation

Skip the outline and flooding, and pipe the snowflake design directly onto the plain cookie.

HOLIDAY PRESENTS

This package cookie cutter is one of my favorites. It's wonderful for holidays, birthdays, or even as a little blue box for engagements.

   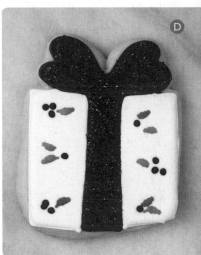

you will need

Vanilla-Almond Sugar Cookies (page 22), present shape

Royal Icing (page 28), divided and tinted:
WHITE • RED

Disposable icing bags (2)

Couplers

Icing tips: #2

Squeeze bottles (2)

Toothpicks

Holly sprinkles

Tweezers

Meringue powder

Small paintbrush

Red sanding sugar

1 Scoop some red and white icings into bags and attach #2 tips.
→ Outline the ribbon on each package in either red or white icing.
→ Outline the edges of each package in the opposite color. Ⓐ

2 Thin the remaining icings of both colors for flooding (as described on page 16). Cover them with a damp dishtowel and let them sit for several minutes. Gently stir with a silicone spatula and transfer icing to squeeze bottles as needed.

3 Fill in the white outlined areas with thinned white icing. Use a toothpick to guide icing to the edges and pop air bubbles.

4 Use tweezers to place holly berries and leaves onto the wet white icing. (Alternately, scatter the sprinkles at random.) Ⓑ

5 Fill in the red outlined areas with the thinned red icing, using a toothpick as before. Ⓒ

6 Let the cookies dry uncovered for 6 to 8 hours or overnight.

7 Mix together ¼ teaspoon meringue powder with ¼ teaspoon water. Brush the red areas with the mixture and sprinkle on red sanding sugar (as described on page 19). Shake off the excess. Ⓓ

8 Let dry for at least 30 minutes.

Variation
Try different color combinations to celebrate many winter holidays: shades of blue are pretty for Hanukkah celebrations; white and ivory capture a certain "new-fallen snow" feel; and glittering silver and gold ring in the new year with style.

MENORAHS

Decked out in shades of blue and gold, these menorah cookies make a festive Hanukkah treat!

you will need

Vanilla-Almond Sugar Cookies
(page 22), menorah shape

Royal Icing (page 28), divided
and tinted:
SKY BLUE • WHITE •
EGG YELLOW • ROYAL BLUE

Disposable icing bags (4)

Couplers

Icing tips: #2, #1

Squeeze bottles (4)

Toothpicks

1 Scoop some sky blue and white icings into bags and attach #2 tips. Outline the menorahs, some with sky blue icing, some with white icing. Reserve some sky blue icing for piping details. Ⓐ

2 Thin the remaining sky blue and white icings for flooding (as described on page 16). Cover the icings with a damp dishtowel and let them sit for several minutes. Gently stir with a silicone spatula and transfer icing to squeeze bottles as needed.

3 Fill in the menorahs with the thinned icing, matching the outline colors. Use a toothpick to guide icing to the edges and pop air bubbles. Let the cookies dry for at least 1 hour.

4 Scoop some yellow and royal blue icings into bags and attach #2 tips.
→ On the light blue cookies, outline the base and candleholders in yellow. Ⓑ
→ On the white cookies, outline the base and candleholders in royal blue.
→ Reserve some of each icing for later piping details.

5 Thin and prepare the remaining yellow and royal blue icings for flooding, and transfer them to squeeze bottles. Fill in the base of the menorahs with the thinned icing, using a toothpick as before. Ⓒ

6 Pipe on the following details:
→ Use a #1 tip with sky blue icing to pipe candles onto the dark blue menorah.
→ Use a #1 tip with royal blue icing to pipe candles onto the yellow menorah.
→ Use a #1 tip with yellow icing to add flames to the candles. Ⓓ

7 Let the cookies dry uncovered for 6 to 8 hours or overnight.

SHIMMER STARS

Simple, shimmering, sparkling stars—they're so pretty throughout the holidays and especially for New Year's Eve!

you will need

Vanilla-Almond Sugar Cookies (page 22), star shapes (see note)

Royal Icing (page 28), divided and tinted:
GOLD • GRAY (MADE USING BLACK)

Disposable icing bags (2)

Couplers

Icing tips: #2

Squeeze bottles (2)

Toothpicks

Gold and silver luster dust

Vodka

Small paintbrushes (2)

Variation
Meringue powder

Small paintbrush

Gold and silver sanding sugar

Note: Before baking, use a small star cookie cutter to cut out the center of larger stars. You can gather the smaller stars into a ball and roll out more dough, or bake both shapes (see the Variation).

1 Scoop some of both icing colors into bags and attach #2 tips. Outline half of the stars with gold icing and the other half with gray. Ⓐ

2 Thin the remaining gold and gray icings for flooding (as described on page 16). Cover the icings with a damp dishtowel and let them sit for several minutes. Gently stir with a silicone spatula and transfer icing to squeeze bottles as needed.

3 Fill in the stars with the thinned icing. Use a toothpick to guide icing to the edges and pop air bubbles. Ⓑ

4 Let the cookies dry uncovered for 6 to 8 hours or overnight.

5 Add luster dust to the stars: In separate containers, mix together $1/4$ teaspoon gold and silver luster dust with several drops of vodka. Brush the mixture onto the stars using a small, clean paintbrush. (Details on applying luster dust are on page 20.) Ⓒ

Variation
Bake the mini stars from the cut-out middles. Outline and flood with gold and gray icing. The next day, mix together $1/4$ teaspoon meringue powder with $1/4$ teaspoon water. Brush the cookies with the mixture and sprinkle on the silver and gold sanding sugar (as described on page 19). Shake off the excess.

GUEST BAKERS

One of the best parts of having a blog is meeting people from all over the world who share the same passion for baking. You know that old saying, to surround yourself with people smarter than you are? Well, I've been lucky enough to do just that. The cookie decorators on the following pages are tremendously talented. I'm thrilled that they are each sharing one of their signature cookie-decorating specialties.

Amanda Rettke

i am baker

www.iambaker.net

i am baker

CONFECTIONS & CREATIONS

Decorating Cookies with Glaze Icing

Instead of royal icing, I use a glaze icing to decorate cookies. Glaze icing doesn't set up quite as hard as royal icing, and it takes a little longer to dry, about 12 to 24 hours. The icing dries with a beautiful, shiny finish.

YOU WILL NEED

- 1 cup powdered sugar
- 1 tablespoon light corn syrup
- 1 drop lemon juice (fresh or processed)
- 1 tablespoon milk
- Flavored extracts (optional)

Combine the powdered sugar, corn syrup, and lemon juice in a bowl.

Add some milk, just a drop at a time. When the icing has reached your desired consistency, spread it on cooled cookies and allow it to dry anywhere from 12 to 24 hours.

Some things to keep in mind:

● If you need a thicker frosting for outlining your cookies, add less milk.

● If you have already outlined your cookies and need to fill them in, add more milk (as much as you need) to make your frosting runny.

● If you are using food coloring, be sure to use less milk. Most food colorings are liquid and can make your frosting runnier. However, if you are using a gel food coloring, your milk quantity can remain the same.

● If you want to add different flavors, you can add drops of vanilla extract, almond extract, lemon extract, or other flavors.

● If you want more shine, use more corn syrup and less milk.

Callye Alvarado

The Sweet Adventures of Sugarbelle
www.sweetsugarbelle.com

Rethinking Cookie Cutters

When I repurpose cookie cutters I begin by imagining the cookie I have in mind and drawing a clear black imaginary line around it. I then take the "outline" and spin it around in my mind until I come up with a simple shape that it resembles. Here are some pointers for your creative process:

● Don't be afraid to sketch. Sit down and sketch out your cookie, then draw a real black line around the sketch. This might help you see unthought-of cutter possibilities.

● Don't be afraid to trim unwanted parts from an unbaked cookie. A flower cutter makes a perfect tutu when cut in half.

● Practice by pulling out your cookie cutters and trying to come up with other things they can be. A moustache can double as a mask with a little flip, a wrapped gift can be a tuxedo … the possibilities are as endless as your imagination. Make a game of it, and have the kids help. And most of all, keep it FUN!

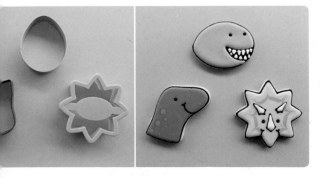

Gail Dosik

One Tough Cookie
www.onetoughcookienyc.com

Adorning Cakes with Cookies

Cookies for the cake are decorated with royal icing and made at least one day in advance so they are perfectly dry. If using stand-up cookies on top, bake lollipop sticks into the cookies, then outline and flood as usual. Cookies are no more than $1/4$ inch thick. Plan out how the cookies are to look on the cake.

The cake has been crumb coated, iced, stacked with the edges decoratively piped, and well chilled. I only use Swiss meringue buttercream for the smoothest finish possible.

Here's how you construct the cake.

1 If working with a tiered cake, adhere the center front cookie on the top tier first, using roughly $1/2$ teaspoon of room-temperature buttercream as "glue." Press gently but firmly for 3 seconds to secure the cookie. If any frosting squeezes out and is visible, use a small, clean, food-safe paintbrush to gently clean up the smear.

TIP *If at any time the buttercream icing on the cake starts to get too soft, refrigerate until firm.*

2 Adhere the center back cookie in the same way. North and South have now been established.

3 Determine the points midway between the front and back cookies to establish East and West. Adhere cookies in the same way.

4 Now fill in between those spaces with cookies. This is the easiest way to space cookies evenly.

5 If doing a second tier, map it out in the same way as the first.

6 Carefully insert the topper cookies last.

7 Chill the cake for at least 10 minutes to set the cookies.

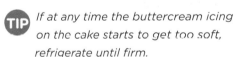

153

Meaghan Mountford

the decorated cookie
www.thedecoratedcookieblog.com

the decorated cookie

Decorating Cookies with Fondant

Fondant is a surprisingly easy and useful decorating tool: it's malleable, so it can be rolled out, cut out, and manipulated, but it stiffens well enough so you can handle and package your cookies easily. For a smooth, finished look, top cookies with fondant instead of royal icing. Or, just use fondant to decorate a cookie with a royal icing base, as shown with these daisy cookie pops.

Rolling and cutting fondant is not much different than what you would do with cookie dough. Briefly knead the fondant to make a ball, flatten it slightly with the palm of your hand, and use a rolling pin to roll the fondant to $1/8$ to $1/4$ inch thick. To prevent sticking, use powdered sugar on your rolling pin and work surface, and lift and move your fondant repeatedly. I lift and turn my fondant with almost every roll of the pin.

TIP *Drops of water make fondant sticky and finicky, so keep your hands and work area very dry. And it only takes one crumb to mar a smooth, clean surface of fondant, so be mindful of runaway crumbs from your cookies.*

Easy Marshmallow Fondant Recipe

YOU WILL NEED

vegetable shortening

2 cups mini marshmallows

2 tablespoons water

2 teaspoons clear vanilla extract*

$3^1/2$ cups powdered sugar, plus more for dusting

*You may substitute regular vanilla extract, but you will need to add extra white food coloring to make a bright white fondant.

Grease a microwave-safe bowl with vegetable shortening. Combine the marshmallows, water, and vanilla in the bowl. Heat the marshmallows in the microwave until they puff a bit, 20 to 30 seconds. Stir well until fully melted and smooth.

Grease the bowl of your standing mixer or a large mixing bowl with vegetable shortening. Put the powdered sugar in the bowl. If using a standing mixer, grease the flat beater well, or grease the beaters of a hand mixer well.

Gradually pour the marshmallow mixture into the sugar and blend well on low speed until a dough forms. If the mixture is too dry and crumbly, add a teaspoon of water. If the mixture is too wet, add $1/4$ cup of powdered sugar.

When you have a good, pliable, doughlike mixture, knead it briefly on a surface dusted with powdered sugar. Wrap the dough in plastic wrap and let it sit for about 30 minutes at room temperature. Store unused fondant at room temperature wrapped very well in plastic wrap.

Making Daisy Cookie Pops

Roll out the chilled cookie dough to about $3/8$ inch thick so the cookies will be thick enough to support a cookie stick. Using a $2^1/2$- to 3-inch circular cookie cutter, cut out the cookies and carefully insert a cookie stick centered in the cookie's thickness and about halfway into the cookie. Arrange the cookies on your baking sheet so the cookies or sticks do not touch each other, and bake them according to the recipe. Let them cool completely.

Outline and flood the cooled cookies with royal icing in any color (the daisy cookie pops were iced in sky blue and electric green). Let the icing set overnight.

Color some of your fondant yellow. Roll out the white fondant and yellow fondant, and use cookie cutters to cut out white daisies and small yellow circles. With dabs of light corn syrup, adhere the yellow circles to the white daisies, and then adhere the daisies to the iced cookies.

Marian Poirier

Sweetopia
www.sweetopia.net

Decorating Cookies with a Projector

If you're in the market to replicate an exact image on a cookie and edible images aren't your cup of tea, you might consider using a projector. Specially made for decorating cakes and cookies, projectors allow the decorator to recreate a design exactly, whether it is from a photograph or a printed template. Images can be minimized or enlarged to fit the size of the cookie, and the light is projected from above, rather than from below, to avoid heating the iced cookie.

By projecting an image onto your cookie, the projector allows you to trace and flood an image exactly, which is great for recreating multiples of the same image. It won't necessarily improve your piping skills, but it will certainly improve your drawing capabilities!

Here are a few ideas for using a projector:

● Decorate cookies with the design and colors of a party invitation

● Copy your team's mascot or logo onto dozens of treats

● Take the guess-work out of piping intricate text or fonts

● Trace photos with precision onto cakes and cookies

Using an Image Projector

Following the instructions included with your particular projector, attach your desired image to the projector head using either the clamps provided or tape (I prefer to use a Kopykake projector for my cookie designs). Project the image onto the cookie and trace the shape in icing. This method makes repeating an image on multiple cookies a breeze, and it takes the guesswork out of drawing freehand.

TEMPLATE

TEMPLATES

Please refer to page 8 for instructions on making cookie cutter templates.

All templates shown at 100% size.

STARS

MUGS OF COCOA

I "HEART" MOM TATTOOS

PUMPKIN PIE

LEMONADE

RECTANGLE
FOR EDIBLE COUPONS

MONOGRAM LETTERS

A B C D E F G H I
J K L M N O P Q
R S T U V W X Y Z

FOR A "POPULAR" TEACHER

Visit www.larkcrafts.com/bonus for a printable template.
This bag topper was created by
Melissa Wilson of www.domesticatedlady.com and
Kate Hadfield of www.katehadfielddesigns.com.

LUCK O' THE IRISH

Visit www.larkcrafts.com/bonus for a printable template.
These images were used with permission from
Amy Locurto of www.livinglocurto.com.

About the Author

Bridget Edwards has been decorating cookies for more than a decade and eating them for as long as she can remember. A self-taught cookie decorator, Bridget started the blog Bake at 350 in 2007 to share the secrets of making beautifully decorated cookies. She lives in Texas with her husband, son, and two kitties.

Visit her blog at www.bakeat350.blogspot.com.

Acknowledgments

Mark, or Mr. E as he is known on the blog . . . you've washed more icing tips and squeeze bottles than any man who's not a pastry chef should ever have to. Thank you, from the bottom of my heart, for being my cookie consultant, best friend, and sweetheart. I thank my lucky stars to have you.

Jack . . . I love that you still want to take cookies to school to share with your friends. Thank you for always helping me "test" the cookie dough. You are one cool cookie; I'd think so even if I weren't your mom.

My wonderful parents . . . Mom, I'm sure you're frantically trying to get a copy of this book in heaven. Thank you for instilling in me a love of lipstick, grammar, and baking for others. Dad, thank you for teaching me to appreciate the simplicity of an oatmeal-raisin cookie.

Molly, my little sister . . . thank you for always offering your support, even while knee-deep in diapers and nursery rhymes. Also, thanks for sharing your Nutella.

Aunt Janice . . . your joy, creativity, and encouragement always inspire me. You were also the very first person to suggest that I write a book. Thank you.

Teresa, Terri, Cheryl, and Amanda . . . you've been my book and cookie cheerleaders. Thank you! Your support means the world to me.

Beth . . . you've held my hand and walked me through this whole writing-a-book thing. Your emails never failed to put a smile on my face, and I'll never look at waxed paper without thinking of you.

Steve . . . thank you for the pictures and your patience, and for putting up with our family for six days.

Ree . . . you are a daily source of inspiration to all food bloggers. Making cookies at the ranch was a day I'll never forget.

Kristen and Terrell . . . thank you for the Starbucks and for eating all of those mistakes.

Amy, Melissa, Kate, and Amanda P. . . . thank you for sharing your creative talents.

Gail, Marian, Amanda, Callye, Meaghan, Shelly, Kristan, Angie, Bea, Renee, Paula, Janet, Laurie, and all of the other cookiers out there . . . thank you for sharing your wisdom and creativity!

Last but not least, the readers of Bake at 350 . . . you all make my day, EVERY day! When I started blogging, I never knew I could have this much fun with just my oven and my computer. Thank you for your love, support, and most of all, for decorating cookies (and gaining a few pounds) right along with me!

Resource Guide

Although most supplies for cookie decorating can be found at your local kitchen supply shop, shopping online can be a lot of fun. You'll find sprinkles and cookie cutters you didn't even know existed and now cannot live without.

Baking Supply Shops

Ateco
www.atecousa.com

Fancy Flours
www.fancyflours.com

Global Sugar Art
www.globalsugarart.com

Layer Cake Shop
www.layercakeshop.com

Sugarcraft
www.sugarcraft.com

Sweet!
www.sweetbakingsupply.com

Wilton
www.wilton.com

Cookie Cutters

Copper Gifts
www.coppergifts.com

H.O. Foose Tinsmithing Co.
www.foosecookiecutters.com

Kitchen Collectables
www.kitchengifts.com

The Little Fox Factory
www.thelittlefoxfactory.com

Craft Stores

A.C. Moore
www.acmoore.com

Hobby Lobby
www.hobbylobby.com

Jo-Ann Fabric and Craft Stores
www.joann.com

Michaels
www.michaels.com

Extracts and Vanilla Beans

Beanilla
www.beanilla.com

Silver Cloud Estates
www.silvercloudestates.com

Icing Printers and Edible-Image Supplies

Kopykake
www.kopykake.com

Sugarcraft
www.sugarcraft.com

Kitchen Supply Shops

King Arthur Flour
www.kingarthurflour.com

Sur la Table
www.surlatable.com

Williams-Sonoma
www.williams-sonoma.com

Packaging and Shipping Supplies

The Container Store
www.containerstore.com

Uline
www.uline.com

INDEX